TAKEOVER!
A Human Rights Approach to Housing

by Cheri Honkala and the Poor People's Army

Copyright © 2024 by the Poor People's Army

All rights reserved.

No portion of this book may be reproduced in any form without written permission from the Poor People's Army, except as permitted by US copyright law.

For the protection of those named and unnamed, some of this book may be true, and some of it may not.

Published in the United States by the Poor People's Press, Philadelphia.

Photographs by Harvey Finkle, Erick Jusino Ortiz, Matt Pillischer, and Joel Severson.

poorpeoplesarmy.org

ISBN: 979-8-9905107-0-8

Printed in the United States of America by:
Fireball Printing
2644-48 Coral Street
Philadelphia, PA 19125

First Edition

Well I went down to the rich man's house
And I took back what he stole from me
I took back my dignity
Took back my humanity.

The Rich Man's House. American traditional labor song adapted by members of the Kensington Welfare Rights Union, which became the Poor People's Army

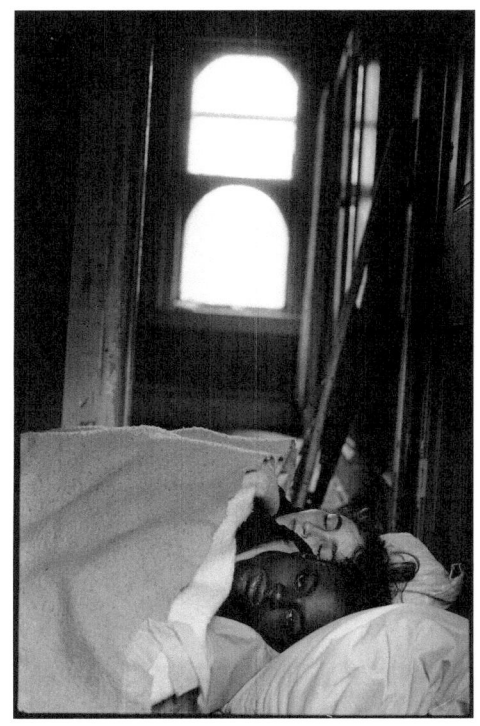

Two homeless members of KWRU sleep in St. Edward's Church as part of the church takeover in September 1995. Photo by Harvey Finkle.

Contents

7 | Introduction
    7 | Call to Movement: The Politics of Love
    13 | About the Poor People's Army
    27 | About This Book
    29 | Context for Our Movement: How the Government Comes to Own Vacant Properties

41 | Chapter 1: The Crew

55 | Chapter 2: Identifying a Target Takeover Home

65 | Chapter 3: Setting Up Utilities and Services

75 | Chapter 4: Orienting Takeover Home Residents

85 | Chapter 5: Moving In, Staying In

101 | Chapter 6: Sustainability, Advocacy, and Movement Building

119 | Appendices
    119 | Appendix A: Takeover Home Location Scouting Checklists
    121 | Appendix B: Takeover Home Resident Memorandum of Understanding
    127 | Appendix C: Media Featuring the Poor People's Army
    137 | Appendix D: Our Philosophy and Perspective on a Changing World (Extended Study Group Version)

Eva and Luisa, children of movement leaders, hold hands at the KWRU Bushville encampment at the RNC in Philadelphia in 2000. Photo by Harvey Finkle.

CALL TO MOVEMENT
The Politics of Love

"I made a choice: I'm not going to die."

Poor People's Army spokesperson Cheri Honkala was torn from her home at the age of 13 when authorities decided her mother, a domestic violence survivor, was too poor to provide for her. After living in nine institutions over three years, Cheri found herself pregnant and unable to pay rent. When the friends she was staying with evicted her, she wrote a check for a white Camaro and lived in it with her young son Mark. Their car was hit by a drunk driver, however, and Cheri and her son were left on the streets. There was nowhere to go; shelter systems were full to capacity and would have separated them by gender as Mark got older. At that moment, Cheri's options were to break the law and house herself and her son, or to die. She chose to live, and not just for herself. Cheri found others in her situation, and on May 1st, 1990, groups of homeless people—most of them women and children—took over vacant houses across the United States. Their attempts to stay alive while poor would become an enduring movement.

There is a lethal disconnect between the promises of our government and the everyday lives of poor people. Right now, according to researcher Elsa Noterman, there are ten abandoned properties for every one homeless person in the city of Philadelphia. Despite this, the wait times to receive public housing are still years long. We have lost beloved community members in the gap between the need for shelter, warmth, and care, and the red tape tying up inadequate government resources. We have witnessed the American dream wash away in the floods of Kensington's factory closures, accumulating back-rents, and the welfare checks that never came. We survived these disasters by sharing, looking out for each other, and showing up. Sometimes this has meant breaking the law in order to get what we need. But we answer to a higher law—that of upholding humanity and securing rights for all people.

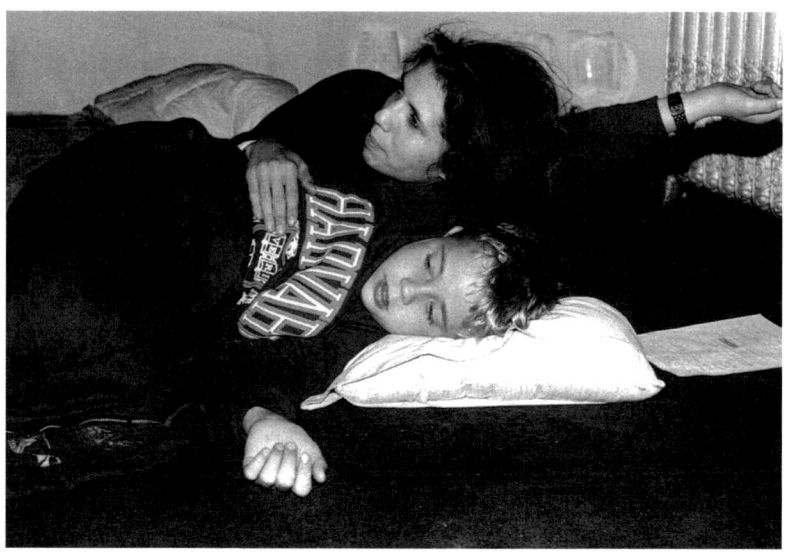

Cheri Honkala embraces her son, Mark Webber, in their first takeover home on 38th Ave in Minneapolis in 1989. Photo by Joel Severson.

This movement for survival became a political movement, even though we never set out to become activists. Our struggle for basic necessities made us an "economic human rights campaign." Our camaraderie as poor people made us an army. But to be clear, there's no romance in poverty. Our movement has lasted so long because our only options are still the same: to get organized or die. We choose life in concrete ways: through housing, food, heat, electricity, baby formula, and diapers. Our "Politics of Love" is the foundation of the better world we are building—one where everyone has what they need without having to fight as hard as we do just to get by.

Choosing the Politics of Love is not easy. The first way we move towards that framework is to acknowledge that we deserve emotional, physical, and social safety. Our needs matter. If they aren't being met, that is not due to a personal failure—the world we were born into was built on stolen lives and labor, and is maintained by violence. We both inflict and endure violence every day, on ourselves and on others, as participants in this system. That violence comes in the form of numbing and disregarding our emotions, turning our time and talents into commodities instead of gifts, and overriding our physical and emotional needs. This isn't normal, natural, or inevitable. A Politics of Love means replacing our resignation with the struggle for liberation. We love each other and we love ourselves, even the parts of ourselves that bend under the weight of oppression. We honor the anger and grief that follow.

Once we build a foundation of self-love as poor people, the next step is to understand that our emotional, physical, and social safety are inseparable from the safety and care of the people around us. We have to break the chains of isolation and individualism every

KWRU members, including Cheri Honkala and Gloria Casarez, take over a Housing and Urban Development Office in 1994. Gloria, then a KWRU intern, went on to be a queer civil rights icon in Philadelphia. Photo by Harvey Finkle.

chance we get. When our neighbor's time, intellect, energy, and creativity are consumed by competitive survival, we suffer too. Who would our community members be if they didn't need to fight to stay afloat every moment of every day? We want to know them, and we want them to know themselves. We want to know ourselves, and have our community see us as whole people. This world is ours to build and the resources already exist to build it; they're just being hoarded by people who profit off of our suffering and the suffering of our planet. People often associate struggle with anger, and we are angry that the world is this way, but what motivates us in our struggle has been and will always be love for ourselves and each other.

That is why we choose to fight together. As poor people, we are taught not to love ourselves. Committing to self-love helps us resist the society that teaches us that we are responsible for our own suffering. As Cheri said in the 2006 documentary *August in the Empire State* (directed by Keefe Murren and Gabriel Rhodes), "don't be ashamed to say that you're poor. I'm poor and I'm proud, but I'm ashamed of my country." We have decided not to die, and we have decided not to let each other die. We do this by "recognizing shared (and uneven) precarity as both a lived reality and organizing principle," as described by scholar Elsa Noterman in her 2020 paper "Taking back vacant property" (see Appendix C for full citation and abstract). We are reclaiming the voice of the poor in the form of a movement for and by poor people, rather than being co-opted or forced to suffer in silence. We believe that vacant federal property belongs to poor people, so we carry out housing takeovers to help them give it back to us. This book is about how to do that.

Cheri Honkala and Galen Tyler join other housing advocates from across the country to protest the US Supreme Court's criminalization of homelessness in 2024. Photo by Erick Jusino Ortiz.

INTRODUCTION
About the Poor People's Army

Our History

We are building a nonviolent Poor People's Army to keep people alive and to build a cooperative economy and society by any means necessary. One of our tactics to keep people alive has always been taking over abandoned houses. This has run through many of the organizations we've founded:

> 1980s: Up & Out of Poverty Now; Women, Work, & Welfare (Minneapolis)
> 1991: Kensington Welfare Rights Union (Philadelphia)
> 1998: Poor People's Economic Human Rights Campaign (National)
> 2018: Poor People's Army (National)

Before we were a national organization, our soldiers began individually taking over abandoned government-owned properties to keep our own families alive in the 1980s. Our leaders founded organizations like Up & Out of Poverty Now and Women, Work, & Welfare in Minneapolis to widen the scope of this work, championing a nationally-coordinated takeover campaign in 1990.

In 1991, a coalition of poor and homeless families helped to establish the Kensington Welfare Rights Union (KWRU) in Philadelphia as part of a national network of welfare rights organizations. KWRU tackled the fallout of welfare cuts, privatization, and rising inequality by organizing dozens of homeless encampments nationwide and hundreds of takeovers of abandoned government-owned homes, as well as military recruitment offices, hospitals, schools, flour mills, factories, and churches—most notably the Saint Edwards Church, documented in both the 1999 book *Myth of the Welfare Queen* by David Zucchino and the 1996 short film *Homeless Diaries* (directed by Frances Negrón-Muntaner). We were also known for our "Ridgeville" encampment in Philadelphia, and an encampment later inside the Harrisburg State Capitol in 1995, where we demanded resources for Pennsylvanians being kicked off welfare.

Soon after those encampments, KWRU began to use a human rights framework based on the United Nations' Universal Declaration of Human Rights. The next year, we planned the first march for human rights using that framework in U.S. history, from the Liberty Bell in Philadelphia to the United Nations in NYC. In 1998, we organized the New Freedom Bus Tour across the U.S., a tactic we have continued to use. Modeled after the 1960s Freedom Summer bus trips that registered people to vote in Mississippi, our tour documented preventable human rights violations in the U.S. and demanded freedom from unemployment, hunger, and homelessness. This work was documented in the 2000 film *Outriders*,

Liz Ortiz and other PPEHRC members demonstrate at the National Housing and Urban Development Office in Washington, D.C. in the early 2000s. Photo by Harvey Finkle.

Cheri Honkala speaks before a million people at the Karnataka Rajya Raitha Sangha demonstration regarding the massive suicide of destitute farmers in India in 2001. Photo by Harvey Finkle.

produced by Pamela Yates and Peter Kinoy. Months later in 1998, we held the Poor People's Summit on Human Rights in Philadelphia and formally established the Poor People's Economic Human Rights Campaign—a national organization of locally focused groups organizing around economic human rights.

Our organization as it exists today, the Poor People's Economic Human Rights Campaign (PPEHRC, AKA Poor People's Army or PPA), is based on the mission of Dr. Martin Luther King, Jr. and others who founded the original Poor People's Campaign in 1968. Like the Poor People's Campaign, PPEHRC is a cross-racial movement to abolish poverty. Our leaders took inspiration from, and were trained by, civil rights and welfare rights organizers of the 1960s, '70s, and '80s. As PPEHRC, we brought charges of human rights violations to the United Nations, and were the first group to assert the human right to housing at the Organization of American States. We have marched on Washington, D.C. and the U.N. countless times. We have used tribunals, conventions, summits, and truth commissions to highlight human rights violations in the U.S. We also helped develop and co-host the United States Social Forum. When our government failed to respond appropriately to natural disasters, such as during Hurricanes Katrina and Maria, and disappeared poor and homeless people away from news cameras, such as during the 2002 Olympics, we mobilized resources to keep people alive and form a unified voice of poor and oppressed people.

During every U.S. presidential election cycle since 2000, PPEHRC has marched with up to 20,000 people at both Democratic and Republican National Conventions—and will do so again in 2024. Some of this work has been documented in *Battle for Broad* (2001, directed by Pamela Yates) and *August in the Empire State*. Throughout this process, we have learned that we cannot wait for corporate parties to develop the political will to care for poor people. We have to take back the basic necessities of life now as we organize for a better society in the future.

Expanding our work internationally, we have shared connections and learnings with other groups who tactically take back their basic necessities as a way to survive, including the Zapatista Army of National Liberation or EZLN (Mexico), the Landless Workers Movement or MST (Brazil), Karnataka Rajya Raitha Sangha or KRRS (India), and La Vía Campesina (particularly their work in Colombia). In 1999, we organized representatives from Central America, South America, and Canada to join PPEHRC on a March of the Americas from Washington, D.C. to the United Nations in New York City. We were accompanied by prominent international Human Rights Observers, including Nora Cortinas of the Mothers of the Plaza de Mayo (Linea Fundadora) of Argentina, Alexis Ponce of the Inter-American Platform for Human Rights, Democracy and Development (from Ecuador), Jan Flaherty of England and many others. We have met with world leaders, including Hugo Chavez (Venezuela), Fidel Castro (Cuba), and Mary Robinson (Ireland). PPEHRC/PPA spokesperson Cheri Honkala was honored to speak at a celebration of Gandhi's birthday in India, addressing a crowd of over a million people. She spoke in India again at the 2004 World Social Forum, which drew over 100,000 participants from around the world. Also in 2004, Front Line—The International Foundation for the Protection of Human Rights Defenders recognized Cheri as one of the human rights organizers most in danger in the world, and gave her amnesty status, should she need it, in the state of Ireland. In 2009, we were included as part of Amnesty International's educational human rights curriculum and featured on video for the organization. Our international travel and networking with poor-led peasants' and workers' movements across the globe brought attention to and supported the organized poor within the United States empire—the belly of the beast.

Like many of these international models, we are not simply advocating on behalf of the poor– we are the poor, organizing and empowering ourselves in a non-violent army: the Poor People's Army. The entirety of this work has been accomplished with shoestring budgets, bank accounts in the negative, and babies on our hips. We have leveraged our relationships and national networks to create events that would even seem impossible to organizations ten times our size. We are focused on building leadership among the poor. We have built leadership in communities across the country who can think for themselves and take collective action in the movement to abolish poverty—led by the people most impacted.

Our housing takeovers use practical solutions for practical problems. We cut through the red tape and provide immediate shelter for ourselves. These tactics act as indictments of the system and also put pressure on those in power to provide long term housing. In addition to advocacy and providing immediate solutions for homelessness, housing takeovers bring poor people together to analyze why human rights violations happen on a daily basis and

PPEHRC members demonstrate at the Philadelphia sheriff's office to stop home foreclosure In 2011. Cheri Honkala (not pictured) was running for sheriff at the time on a platform of zero evictions.
Photo by Harvey Finkle.

bring attention to the conditions that are hidden by the media and ignored by politicians. These actions are central to our organization for today's world. They also challenge people to think of how we could organize a better world.

Our Political Context and Philosophy

"The only real revolutionary, people say, is a man who has nothing to lose. There are millions of poor people in this country who have very little, or even nothing, to lose. If they can be helped to take action together, they will do so with a freedom and a power that will be a new and unsettling force in our complacent national life."

-Dr. Martin Luther King Jr., "Nonviolence and Social Change," 1967

We take over houses because we are in the midst of a battle for our futures. An increasingly small and powerful group of the ultra-rich hoard astronomical wealth, and along with it the power to dictate how society is run. This is not a conspiratorial, shadowy group of figures—the names of these men are publicly available. According to Forbes' 2024 Billionaires List, the 14 richest people in the world have over $100 billion *each*. These are their names: Bernard Arnault of France, Elon Musk of the United States, Jeff Bezos of the United States, Mark Zuckerberg of the United States, Larry Ellison of the United States, Warren Buffett of the United States, Bill Gates of the United States, Steve Ballmer of the United States, Mukesh Ambani of India, Larry Page of the United States, Sergey Brin of the United States, Michael Bloomberg of the United States, Amancio Ortega of Spain, and Carlos Slim Helú of Mexico.

Imagine the problems that could be solved with $100 billion. Instead, these men and other members of the ultra-rich control the economy and our destinies by making decisions about how much food is grown, how housing markets operate, and how the healthcare system runs. They help write laws and use their money and power to undermine our so-called democracy. They have bought out and corporatized the media and culture that shapes our perception of what's possible. They control our employment and remind us that we are replaceable when cheaper labor or automation is possible instead.

Meanwhile, the vast majority of Americans do not own corporations. We do not own businesses that can decide how food and medicines are made, how housing is planned, how water is kept clean, or how educational resources are created for our children. Most Americans have to work to survive, run small businesses or "side hustles," or use other means to get their basic needs met. According to "The State of U.S. Wealth Inequality," a 2023 report conducted by the Federal Reserve Bank of St. Louis, these people—the bottom 50%—control less than 3% of the wealth. In fact, the bottom 90% control little more than 30% of the wealth. This system—the ruling class exploiting the working class—is the bedrock of capitalism.

Capitalism is a violent system. Poor and working people suffer at the hands of the police, the courts, prisons, and detention centers. We endure violence from a healthcare system that excludes us, that ignores our mental health, that treats our addictions and sorrows as personal failures. We endure violence from social workers and systems put in place to criminalize poverty and punish poor parents by breaking up families, by removing children from their homes, by imprisoning and punishing poor parents and caregivers. Our water, air, and soil are poisoned, causing mass extinction and climate catastrophe borne disproportionately by the poor and working class.

In order to tackle these problems, we can't just fight back against isolated disastrous changes or organize in silos. Instead, we must focus on collective solutions that revolutionize the control of how goods are produced, distributed, and shared. We highlight contradictions of inequality by taking back empty houses for homeless people, taking back empty land for our communities' use, and distributing free food. We decry the disconnect of our government spending billions of dollars on wars while defunding change at home. We call out politicians' hypocrisy when they impose sanctions to regimes abroad without recognizing their own sanctions against poor and working people in the U.S. through the denial of benefits and the withholding of basic necessities of life.

We understand that poor and working people must find a way to unite during the difficult transition that lies in the years ahead. We also know that it will take organizing to build the forces capable of ultimately getting rid of inequality. We need to meet people where they're at, and catch people when they're down. We build unity by helping people when they are thrown out of the system—when they are outsourced, downsized, and kicked out of their homes. We do our best to assist people when they can't get access to decent healthcare or detox on demand, when they are bankrupted by hospital bills or denied treatment by insurance companies. We are there when they can't reunite with their children, or the state is threatening to take their kids away simply because they are poor. These are our people. If we can grow our consciousness together, then we can transform society. We can break down the false political ideologies of "liberal" and "conservative" used to divide us, and unify the bottom to come for the top.

We are the leaders that we are looking for. Let's seize this moment.

Principles of Unity

The following Principles of Unity were established democratically by poor people organizing themselves, and are principles by which the Poor People's Army functions:

1. We support and lift up poor people's leadership. If problems arise, we agree to sit down and find resolution in order to move forward for the best interest of the movement.

2. We identify and address the root causes of our poverty.

3. We support the international poor people's movement as we work locally.

4. We are building a movement that enacts the future we want to see—one based on a cooperative economy and society.

5. We organize for power. This means embracing tactics and strategies that help move the movement towards political independence. We are interested in enacting an alternative paradigm framed on the needs of the movement rather than those of corporate-controlled political parties.

6. We are committed to peace even as we daily suffer violence—the violence of unemployment, hunger, and homelessness. We have a right to feed, clothe and house our families—this is not up for negotiation. We also have a right to speak for ourselves about these inhuman conditions in which we live and have a responsibility to shed light on those that benefit both directly and indirectly from our collective misery.

7. We have a right and a duty to protect our families and each other.

8. We are collectively creating our vision for a different kind of world. We commit ourselves to daily political education, and do not take our leadership roles lightly. We will not allow ourselves to be bought or co-opted.

9. We are committed to making and controlling our own media.

10. We recognize the need for a radical break with the status quo of progressive politics. We can no longer afford to hold onto old models of organizing that do not challenge capitalism. We must actively seek a significant paradigm shift, looking to other peasant models in the rest of the world and organize across borders.

11. We recognize the intersectionality of our oppression. Racism, classism, sexism, xenophobia, homophobia, ableism, and trans-

Leaders of Karnataka Rajya Raitha Sangha in India express solidarity with KWRU in 2001. Photo by Harvey Finkle.

phobia intersect in the ways we experience daily violence. However, we will not allow the police, social workers, doctors, scholars, clergy, nonprofits, or political parties to divide us along these lines.

12. We know the entire global capitalist economy is disrupted and undermined as new laborless electronic technology is applied to production, permanently replacing hundreds of millions of workers. These workers are cast out of, or to the margins of the economy, with little or no ability to buy the necessities of life. These workers are a new class created by robot/AI production. Our job is to build unity among this new class based on common poverty.

13. We acknowledge that this country was built on white supremacy, imperialism, colonialism, and militarism, and we resist the ongoing perpetuation of these systems of violence.

14. Our work breaks with the military, prison, nonprofit, and faith industrial complexes.

15. We honor our ancestors, lifting up their histories and work so we may learn from them and share their knowledge with the generations to come.

16. We are building poor and working class political leadership and representation. We can no longer afford to have our movements used as the "base" of the Democratic and Republican parties—especially at a time when the political elite of both parties are directly or indirectly participating in the diminishment of workers' rights.

BACKGROUND

About This Book

This resource is the result of a years-long, cross-class collaboration between the Poor People's Army leadership and a group of young people with wealth and/or class privilege belonging to the Philadelphia chapter of Resource Generation ("RG Philly"), who contributed time, labor, and funds to make this book a reality. Resource Generation defines itself as a national organization mobilizing young people 18-35 years old with wealth to redistribute money, land, and power (learn more at resourcegeneration.org).

The idea for this book arose over lunch in the summer of 2022, when Cheri and an RG member-leader met to brainstorm ways to resource the Poor People's Army. Through a series of interviews, coworking sessions, and skill sharing from many supporters, three decades' worth of wisdom and organizing was distilled into this guide. It is intended to support poor people, whose leadership is critical to providing immediate material solutions to homelessness as well as large-scale changes from organized advocacy.

The following chapters contain practical step-by-step descriptions of how we approach all aspects of taking over a home. The first chapter discusses how we find collaborators and all the skill sets that are useful for a crew to possess. The second chapter explains how we find vacant government-owned properties to turn into takeover homes. Chapter 3 lays out the process for establishing necessary services so that the home is safe and functional. In the fourth chapter, we outline how to support housing seekers who may become residents of takeover homes. Chapter 5 describes move-in day and how the crew can help the new takeover home residents settle in. The sixth chapter widens the scope of the discussion to longer-term infrastructure and interactions with institutions such as the legal system, the media, and the nonprofit industrial complex. Finally, the appendix contains additional resources including helpful checklists, sample contract language, media featuring the Poor People's Army and our members, and an extended version of our philosophy and political analysis intended for use by study groups.

CONTEXT FOR OUR MOVEMENT

How the Government Comes to Own Vacant Properties

This piece was written in solidarity by a local scholar and friend to the Poor People's Army.

Laws allowing the city to take over houses

Houses usually end up being owned by HUD, the federal Department of Housing and Urban Development, when an FHA-insured mortgage is not paid. The FHA (Federal Housing Authority) insures most mortgages on homes.[1] When someone can't pay their mortgage, the bank or mortgage lender forecloses on the house and tries to sell it in a foreclosure sale to get their money back. They can also get a court order to have the property auctioned off in a sheriff's sale. If they can't sell it for enough money, they can give the house to HUD to get their insurance money from the FHA instead. HUD puts those houses up for sale on their website, www.hudhomestore.gov). If the houses don't sell within six months and cost less than $25,000, the houses can be sold to local governments or registered nonprofits for $1.[2] In 1989, George H.W. Bush's new secretary of HUD, Jack Kemp, promised to help solve the affordable housing crisis by giving 10% of HUD homes to homeless people, but few homes were actually given out—instead, some HUD-approved sponsors like religious leaders basically got free houses.[3]

The Kensington Welfare Rights Union (KWRU) occupied HUD-owned homes in 1994 through takeovers.[4] In response, the HUD office in Philadelphia sent a letter to one of the homes which said: "This property is not habitable in its current condition. There are various code violations present, all utilities are inactive and have not been tested for safety, a lead-based paint hazard exists, and the overall disrepair of the home represents a danger. Therefore, your occupancy presents a health, safety, and fire hazard to you and the adjoining property owners."[5] The houses were up for sale and had real estate agents, but they had to be fixed up and inspected before they could be legally rented out or lived in. This letter points out real dangers to the occupant of the house as well as the property owners next door. But is being in a house with lead paint or repair problems more dangerous than being unhoused? Is owning property next to a takeover home more dangerous than owning property next to a vacant building?

City governments also own houses, many of which are vacant with no one living in them.[6] These vacant units are officially uninhabitable—they are not in good enough condition to live in. The Philadelphia Code—our city's code of laws and regulations—allows the city to take over vacant or "surplus" properties. The law exists to fix the problem of "blight." Blight is another word for disease (like the disease that killed potato plants and led to the Great Hunger in Ireland), and a blighted area of a city is definitely unhealthy, although the causes of urban blight are not natural. Blighted areas discourage new people or businesses from coming to the city.[7] There aren't people paying property taxes or running businesses that bring money in for the city. A 2010 study found that the City of Philadelphia spends about $20 million a year on vacant properties (including the ones it doesn't own), when you count things like trash cleanup, pest control, fire department calls, policing, etc.[8] So the city sees it as being in the public interest, or for the good of the whole city and its ability to use taxes to pay for public services, to do something to fix blight. That usually begins with the city taking over ownership of properties in blighted areas. According to the Philadelphia Code, blighted properties can include those that are dilapidated, unsanitary, infested with vermin, or hazardous, but also those where the utilities have been shut off or which are sitting vacant or have unpaid taxes. The full text of the relevant Philadelphia Code sections is included at the end of this section.

The contradiction of "urban blight"

In response to a Right to Know Law Request in April 2023, the Philadelphia Housing Authority (PHA) reported owning 515 vacant units, while 56,144 people sit on their waiting list for housing.[9] But organizers say the reality is that the PHA has many more vacant units than that, and in a 2021 article in *Philadelphia* magazine, reporter Nate File said the PHA owned more than 5,000 vacant properties, and had over 86,000 people on its waiting list.[10]

The Philadelphia code assumes that urban blight is a threat to public welfare: it makes people sick and unsafe to have a lot of uninhabitable units around, and it costs the city money. However, by holding onto vacant units without making them habitable—or giving them to families who will make them habitable—the city is actually now perpetuating urban blight and all the problems that come with it. Even calling these properties "surplus" in the city code is insulting to people who need a roof over their heads—or to the 56,000 people on the Philadelphia Housing Authority's waitlist. A Pew Charitable Trusts article also talks about a very different kind of vacant property: the empty homes owned by rich people who don't even live in them.[11] The city has never yet used its authority to take over that kind of vacant property for the "public good."

The Philadelphia Housing Authority can't move tenants into a property until it passes inspection as "habitable," and the PHA says it doesn't have enough money to fix up vacant properties it owns to meet that standard. Kelvin Jeremiah, the president and CEO of PHA, says it costs $100,000 to over $250,000 to fix up a single vacant house.[12] But organizers say that the rehab can be done at a much lower cost, especially when families can move in and take care of fixing up their own home themselves. Jeremiah's salary as of 2017 was $263,153.98.[13] A 2020 article reports that PHA raised money to fix up 1800 units and make them habitable by auctioning off more than 500 properties to the highest bidder, but the PHA reports that their last property auction was in 2019, so it's unclear if the PHA has continued to try to raise funds this way.[14]

One section of the city code, Section 16-404, dictates how the PHA is able to sell or transfer ownership of vacant properties. Individuals can apply to the city to buy vacant properties, as long as "the applicant has no City tax or water delinquencies, or other City delinquencies," and doesn't own any properties with current violations. The city has to sell properties in a competitive process open to multiple bidders, advertising when a property is available and selecting the best bid according to a formula. Only 5% of the formula has to do with how much money the applicant is offering. This competitive process is supposed to prevent corruption: a city council member cannot just give a property to whoever they want, according to the rules, although organizers have found council members doing just that.

A failed agreement to transfer vacant properties

Early in the COVID pandemic, in June 2020, groups including the Workers Revolutionary Collective (WRC), and #OccupyPHA came together to set up two encampments for unhoused people. The first encampment, Camp JTD (named for James Talib-Dean, a co-founder of WRC who passed away in June 2020), was set up on the Benjamin Franklin Parkway in front of the Philadelphia Museum of Art. #OccupyPHA Camp Teddy (named for Teddy, a 60-year-old unhoused man who had been living in an encampment at the airport cleared by police in March 2020) was set up on the brand new $45 million campus of the Philadelphia Housing Authority on Fairmount Ave. The organizers also set up housing takeovers at 11 properties.[15]

The city tried to evict people from the encampments three times, and finally made an agreement with the organizers on October 12, which included the transfer of 50 vacant properties from city ownership to the Community Land Trust in Philadelphia to become permanently affordable housing, and also allowed families to stay in the takeover homes.[16] Reporter Darryl Murphy said the agreement "echoes a deal made in 1987, when housing activists took over 14 city-owned homes to protest homelessness and convinced then-Mayor Wilson Goode to fork over about 200 city-owned homes to a nonprofit called Dignity Housing that still exists today."[17] Seven homes in Strawberry Mansion were designated to be rehabbed by people from the encampment themselves after they received training from the city's Building and Construction Trades Council.[18] However, as of July 2023, years later, none of those vacant properties have been transferred.

History of "surplus properties" law

The original Surplus Properties ordinance in Philadelphia was passed in 1973. After World War II, in the 1950s, Philadelphia and many other cities in the US were actually losing population and businesses as residents—especially white residents—left to live in the fashionable new suburbs you see in old sitcoms (this migration is often called "white flight"). In 1960, the city had about 2,002,512 residents; in 1970, that number declined to 1,948,609; in 1980, 1,688,210; in 1990, 1,585,577.[19] The cities were losing so much tax revenue as a result that their governments began an "urban renewal" movement to try to draw wealthy residents and businesses back in. To build new shopping centers, apartment buildings, and parks in search of "renewal," they cleared "blighted" areas. This included slums, tenements, and dilapidated homes. It also included homes and buildings that were seen as "in the way" of a more desirable use for that land. In the early 1900s, for example, Philadelphia city planners wanted to beautify the city by building the Benjamin Franklin Parkway, and a Vacant Property Research Network report notes that "the Parkway cut through a dense working-class neighborhood and only worsened the city's shortage of decent, affordable housing."[20] Urban renewal was never designed to benefit the people living in "blighted" areas. Recently, the 2008-2009 foreclosure crisis forced more people to abandon their homes and caused "blighted" areas to grow again.

In 1954, the same year the Supreme Court heard the *Brown vs. Board of Education* case and mandated school integration in the South, the court also heard another case, *Berman vs. Parker*. Max Morris, a man whose department store in Washington, D.C. was taken by eminent domain[21] by the District of Columbia Redevelopment Land Agency, sued the agency, saying that his store wasn't blighted at all—even if houses around it were—so it didn't serve the public good to take it away from him. The Supreme Court justices sided with the city, saying that seizing the grocery store was going to help to remedy the overall blight in the area.[22] That pattern continues today. In 2016, for example, the Philadelphia Housing Authority demolished the Norman Blumberg Housing complex in Sharswood, and as part of their plan for "renewal" in the area, they also acquired "1,300 neighborhood properties, 800 of which are privately owned, through eminent domain." All but 73 of those were vacant, according to the city.[23]

Philadelphia Code

Section 16-503 of the Philadelphia Code defines 8 kinds of blighted properties:

" (1)   Blighted property shall include:

(a)   Any premises which because of physical condition or use is regarded as a public nuisance at common law or has been declared a public nuisance in accordance with the provisions of this Code.

(b)   Any premises which because of physical condition, use or occupancy is considered an attractive nuisance to children, including but not limited to abandoned wells, shafts, basements, excavations, and unsafe fences or structures.

(c)   Any dwelling which because it is dilapidated, unsanitary, unsafe, vermin-infested or lacking in the facilities and equipment required by this Code, has been designated as unfit for human habitation.

(d)   Any structure which is a fire hazard, or is otherwise dangerous to the safety of persons or property.

(e)   Any structure from which the utilities, plumbing, heating, sewerage or other facilities have been disconnected, destroyed, removed, or rendered ineffective so that the property is unfit for its intended use.

(f)   Any vacant or unimproved lot or parcel of ground in a predominantly built-up-neighborhood, which by reason of neglect or lack of maintenance has become a place for accumulation of trash and debris, or a haven for rodents or other vermin.

(g)   Any unoccupied property which has been tax delinquent for a period of two years.

(h)   Any property which is vacant but not tax delinquent, which has not been rehabilitated within one year of the receipt of notice issued under this Code to rehabilitate."[24]

The beginning of section 16-400 of the Philadelphia Code, entitled "Surplus Properties," explains what the city should do with vacant properties that fit one of these categories, and why the city should take ownership of them:

"The Council of the City of Philadelphia hereby finds that:

(1) Throughout the City of Philadelphia a large number of properties are vacant and have been vacant for an abnormal amount of time;

(2) The vacant properties are in such poor physical condition as to make them uninhabitable in the present conditions;

(3) Certain properties have been declared by City to be unfit for human habitation since they are in violation of building, fire, health and other City Codes;

(4) The owners of certain vacant or unoccupied properties are delinquent in the payment of Real Estate Taxes, Water and Sewer Rents, or other municipal liens and charges;

(5) The properties in their present conditions are and have become a blighting influence in and about the neighborhood where located and thus are a liability to the City and its citizenry;

(6) Nonpayment of the tax obligations by the owners of these properties indicates that they may have or intend to abandon such properties;

(7) Certain property owners desire to donate properties to the City as an alternative to abandoning them;

(8) It would be in the best interest of the owners of such properties and the citizens of Philadelphia if such property would be acquired, and accepted by the City of Philadelphia, to be held in trust until they can be rehabilitated for use by its citizens under certain terms and conditions;

(9) The City has acquired a number of vacant properties throughout the City at Sheriff's sales within its equity of unpaid taxes. Certain of these properties are surplus to the needs of the City but are capable of being improved, rehabilitated and re-used by the citi-

zens of Philadelphia. Inasmuch as the City has no bonded indebtedness invested in these properties and their re-use will relieve the City of the care, maintenance and management of the properties, arrest the blight of the neighborhoods within which they are located and restore the properties to productive use, certain of these properties should be made available for disposition in accordance with the provisions of this Chapter;

(10) Certain other vacant properties cannot be acquired by donation either due to inability to locate the owners, heirs or successors in title; title vests in insolvent estates, institutions or corporations; defects exist in the chain of title; or claims of other than municipal creditors such as mortgagees, judgment or lien holders either cannot or will not be released or satisfied of record insofar as they affect title to such properties thereby deeming acquisition by Eminent Domain essential and serving a public purpose which will promote the public health, safety and welfare."[25]

Endnotes

1. About Us" FHA page on HUD website. https://www.hud.gov/program_offices/housing/fhahistory.
2. "About Dollar Homes," HUD website. https://www.hud.gov/program_offices/housing/sfh/reo/goodn/dhmabout.
3. April 2, 1990. "Report Cites Church Leaders' Abuse of H.U.D.," *New York Times*. https://www.nytimes.com/1990/12/02/us/report-cites-church-leaders-abuse-of-hud.html
4. In 1994, when the Kensington Welfare Rights Union took over HUD homes, a HUD representative criticized KWRU for not buying the homes for $1 and running them as transitional housing. However, KWRU would have had to go through a costly process to register as a nonprofit and then taken on all the costs of running transitional housing according to official procedures, and those costs were too high to be practical.
5. David Zucchino (1997). *Myth of the welfare queen: a Pulitzer prize-winning journalist's portrait of women on the line*. Scribner. pp. 303, 309.
6. The City of Philadelphia now has an open data project to show a map of "likely vacant" properties, mostly so that developers can buy them. They make the map

by gathering information on which properties have code violations, disconnected utilities, or missing payments or licenses. Elsa Noterman (2022), "Speculating on vacancy." *Transactions of the Institute of British Geographers* 47:123–138.

7. Erwin de Leon and Joseph Schilling (April 2017), "Urban Blight and Public Health: Addressing the Impact of Substandard Housing, Abandoned Buildings, and Vacant Lots." Urban Institute research report. https://www.urban.org/sites/default/files/publication/89491/2017.04.03_urban_blight_and_public_health_vprn_report_finalized.pdf; Joseph Schilling and Jimena Pinzón (2016), "The Basics of Blight: Recent Research on Its Drivers, Impacts, and Interventions." Vacant Property Research Network. https://vacantpropertyresearch.com/wp-content/uploads/2016/03/20160126_Blight_FINAL.pdf

8. Econsult Corporation, Penn Institute for Urban Research, and May 8 Consulting. 2010. "Vacant Land Management in Philadelphia: The Costs of the Current System and the Benefits of Reform," Redevelopment Authority of the City of Philadelphia, https://econsultsolutions.com/wp-content/uploads/2010/09/Vacant-Land-Reform-Analysis-FINAL-REPORT_2010-09-23.pdf

9. Right to Know Law Request filed by the author with the Philadelphia Housing Authority, March 7, 2023, and fulfilled April 13, 2023. https://www.pha.phila.gov/contact/right-to-know/

10. Nate File, October 9, 2021, "Philly's Housing Encampments of 2020 Led to a Nationally Celebrated Deal. Then It All Began to Unravel." *Philadelphia* magazine. https://www.phillymag.com/news/2021/10/09/parkway-encampments-housing-agreement/

11. Tim Henderson, November 22, 2022, "The Nation's Vacant Homes Present an Opportunity — and a Problem." *Stateline*, Pew Charitable Trusts. https://www.pewtrusts.org/en/research-and-analysis/blogs/stateline/2022/11/22/the-nations-vacant-homes-present-an-opportunity-and-a-problem

12. Darryl C. Murphy, October 26, 2020, "9 rehabbed homes and a test of radical housing activism are coming to this block." *PlanPhilly*, WHYY. https://whyy.org/articles/9-rehabbed-homes-and-a-test-of-radical-housing-activism-are-coming-to-this-block/

13. Philadelphia Inquirer DataHub. https://data.philly.com/philly/PHA/payroll/.

14. Darryl C. Murphy, October 26, 2020, "9 rehabbed homes and a test of radical housing activism are coming to this block." *PlanPhilly*, WHYY. https://whyy.org/articles/9-rehabbed-homes-and-a-test-of-radical-housing-activism-are-coming-to-this-block/

15. Samantha Melamed, August 5, 2020, "Once-homeless Philly families are squatting in PHA houses. The agency wants them out." *Philadelphia Inquirer.* https://www.inquirer.com/news/pha-squatters-homeless-vacant-houses-20200805.html

16. Darryl C. Murphy, October 5, 2020, "City, activists come to agreement to clear Ridge Avenue homeless encampment." *PlanPhilly*, WHYY. https://whyy.

org/articles/one-of-two-homeless-encampments-comes-to-an-agreement-with-the-city-to-disband/; Max Marin, February 23, 2021, "Inside Philly's 40-year war on homeless encampments." *Billy Penn* at WHYY. https://billypenn.com/2021/02/23/philadelphia-homeless-encampment-parkway-chris-sprowal-mayor-goode-kenney/; Jason N. Peters, December 14, 2020, "The homeless of Philadelphia acted collectively, and got results." *Grid* magazine. https://gridphilly.com/blog-home/2020/12/14/the-homeless-of-philadelphia-acted-collectively-and-got-results/

17. Darryl C. Murphy, October 26, 2020, "9 rehabbed homes and a test of radical housing activism are coming to this block." *PlanPhilly*, WHYY. https://whyy.org/articles/9-rehabbed-homes-and-a-test-of-radical-housing-activism-are-coming-to-this-block/

18. ibid.

19. US Census "Fast Facts." https://www.census.gov/history/www/through_the_decades/fast_facts/

20. Joseph Schilling and Jimena Pinzón, 2016, "The Basics of Blight: Recent Research on Its Drivers, Impacts, and Interventions." Vacant Property Research Network. https://vacantpropertyresearch.com/wp-content/uploads/2016/03/20160126_Blight_FINAL.pdf

21. The Fifth Amendment of the Bill of Rights in the US Constitution includes a section that says, "nor shall private property be taken for public use, without just compensation." A government's power to take away private property is sometimes called "eminent domain," from a Latin term for "supreme ownership" – this refers to the principle that the government's ownership of land is supreme over private ownership of land, in some legal systems.

22. Lavine, Amy. (2010). "Urban Renewal and the Story of Berman v. Parker." The Urban Lawyer, 42(2), 423–475. http://www.jstor.org/stable/27895791.

23. Ashley Hahn, February 22, 2016, "Remaking Sharswood." *PlanPhilly* for WHYY. https://whyy.org/articles/remaking-sharswood/

24. https://codelibrary.amlegal.com/codes/philadelphia/latest/philadelphia_pa/0-0-0-295061

25. https://codelibrary.amlegal.com/codes/philadelphia/latest/philadelphia_pa/0-0-0-294957

CHAPTER 1

The Crew

A successful home takeover requires a dedicated community group of people with a wide range of skills and qualities. Referred to hereafter as "the crew," those who take over houses must trust one another to collectively navigate the risks involved in the takeover process. This chapter will outline the roles for takeover home crew members and provide guidance for how to work together in long-term solidarity.

Recruitment

Initially, finding people to join a housing takeover crew is largely an exercise in underground social networking. This networking should start with close, existing relationships and expand out through family and social networks. When we in the Poor People's Army are approaching a new recruit, we start by having a conversation about what it is that we do and why—namely, that we take over unoccupied government-owned houses and make them safe for homeless families to live in, because there are people dying on the streets who need them.

Holding regular political education sessions that are open to the public is another useful recruitment tool. In these sessions, crew members can explain the ideological and political foundations of the work, as well as provide an overview of the takeover process and ways people can get involved. More information about how the Poor People's Army provides political education is available in Chapter 6.

Finally, word of mouth is a powerful draw. Many of our crew members live or used to live in a takeover home, or know someone who did. Others come to us for support with food or clothing and stick around to help. Still others, including members of the faith community, give donations of clothing or housewares and want to get more involved upon learning more about our work.

Crew Member Roles

Many skills are needed to take over a home. Despite the various tasks and types of expertise required, this essential human rights work can happen using only a few crew members and whatever resources can be scrounged. After all, this is work of necessity—if we always had everything we needed, we wouldn't have to do this at all.

At the center of the mission is the leadership team. This small group of two to five core crew members must coordinate the housing takeovers while participating in them themselves. Deep trust gained from being in long-term personal and/or organizing relationships should bind this group as a foundational bedrock of safety and support. The size of this core can grow or shrink with the volume of takeovers and should incorporate new leaders periodically in the interest of health and sustainability.

Members of the leadership team should be homeless, formerly homeless, and/or poor people, all with roots in the area of the takeover home(s). Previous experience with nonviolent civil disobedience, direct action, conflict mediation and resolution, project management, relationship-building, and communication will be helpful. Personality characteristics such as integrity, creativity, and charisma will also be valuable.

Beyond the leadership team, the following charts outline an aspirational set of roles for a fully developed housing takeover organization. Roles are separated out below for the sake of clarity—in practice, though, members of the Poor People's Army frequently contribute in multiple areas and share expertise with each other in order to remain adaptable. Fluid structures and overlapping duties also help frustrate attempts at surveillance from the state.

What's Needed

BASIC FUNCTIONS

ROLE	DESCRIPTION & QUALIFICATIONS	SPECIFIC RESPONSIBILITIES
Fundraisers / Treasurer(s) / Fiscal Sponsor Liaison(s)	While houses can be taken over on a shoestring budget, expenses will inevitably arise. Fundraising is a constant need. Once raised, money needs to be managed and disbursed. Management and disbursement can be separated or combined. This person/people will likely also be part of the core leadership team.	Fundraise for: • Rent for headquarters • Storage units for spare furniture and belongings • Food and supplies • Takeover home repairs • Home furnishings and appliances • Services and labor (legal, electrical, plumbing, painting, moving, transportation, events) Track budget and expenses Coordinate with fiscal sponsor if applicable (see Chapter 6)
Intake Counselor(s)	Intake counselors talk to people who come to the Poor People's Army seeking shelter. They should be a compassionate, credible, and knowledgeable partner in the person's efforts to navigate an emotionally and materially difficult situation. Sharing personal experience with homelessness is one way a counselor can establish trust, so homeless or formerly homeless crew members are good candidates to carry out intake counseling. Knowledge of government and local services will also help facilitate a smooth crisis resolution process.	Listen to housing seekers' stories without judgment Help housing seekers understand their options Begin meeting immediate material needs such as food, and assuring the potential takeover home resident that they (and often their family) will have a place to sleep that night Coordinate to ensure that the person exhausts all "official" options for housing (see Chapter 4)

BASIC FUNCTIONS, CT'D

ROLE	DESCRIPTION & QUALIFICATIONS	SPECIFIC RESPONSIBILITIES
Location Scout(s)	Location scouts identify government-owned properties that are good candidates to become takeover homes. A location scout needs to know what makes a good takeover home and have a strong working knowledge of the local social and political landscape, since these considerations feature heavily into the viability of a home. Access to an inconspicuous car and a driver's license are helpful. Location scouts should also have an inconspicuous appearance and manner, and a good eye for detail. Prior experience in contracting, architecture, or ability to spot structural issues is a bonus.	Identify good takeover home candidates through government websites or neighborhood visits. Investigate addresses to evaluate current ownership, likelihood of being targeted for developer purchase, and other liabilities that could shorten the life of the takeover home (see Chapter 2) Inspect property (see Chapter 2)

PREPARING PROPERTIES

ROLE	DESCRIPTION & QUALIFICATIONS	SPECIFIC RESPONSIBILITIES
Locksmith	When fixing up and moving into a home, the rest of the crew needs to be able to use a key to walk through the front door. Locksmiths who can perform this service should be certified to work in the area and able to execute the task confidentially.	Discreetly change locks on target homes before repairs and move-in day
Electrician	Securing access to electrical utilities and ensuring safety are critical parts of the move-in process. If repairs would be too extensive in order to make a property habitable, the electrician should be prepared to say that the team should look for a different home. An electrician on the team should be discreet and certified to work in the area.	Turn on electrical services (see Chapter 3) Ensure safety of electrical systems Make any necessary repairs
Plumber / Water Liberator	Turning on water to the house will be critical before families move in. Licensed plumbers can inspect the property and ensure habitability. Extensive repairs may deem a property too expensive to take over.	Turn on water from the street (see Chapter 3) Ensure taps are working and no leaks are evident Make any necessary repairs
Painter	Lead paint is a major issue for families with children and pets.	Check for lead paint and paint over it if it is detected

PREPARING PROPERTIES, CT'D

ROLE	DESCRIPTION & QUALIFICATIONS	SPECIFIC RESPONSIBILITIES
Cleaners	Takeover homes often need to be emptied of trash and abandoned belongings. If the amount of cleaning appears daunting, bring in additional hands to lighten the load. Cleaners should be physically capable of bending and lifting and have access to cleaning supplies and personal protective equipment such as gloves and masks.	Clean target takeover home prior to move-in day

Galen Tyler, formerly homeless father, veteran, and leader in the Poor People's Army, helps a family move into a takeover home in 1998. Photo by Harvey Finkle.

PUBLIC RELATIONS

ROLE	DESCRIPTION & QUALIFICATIONS	SPECIFIC RESPONSIBILITIES
Attorney	Housing takeover work intersects with housing and civil rights law, which means lawyers are crucial partners for crew members and residents. Ideally, a housing attorney would provide pro bono services, but it can be difficult to secure legal support from someone who specializes in housing law and is able to work for free. Lawyers who support the crew should at least be qualified to practice in the jurisdiction in which the takeovers are occurring.	Legal observation on move-in days Jail support Prepare and file affidavits (see Chapter 6) Work with core team, takeover families/residents, and media spokesperson to bring lawsuits against government agencies and police departments

PPA leaders Cheri Honkala, Galen Tyler, and Nick Carmack protest the 76ers arena building project and the displacement of residents of Philadelphia's Chinatown in 2023. Photo by Erick Jusino Ortiz.

PUBLIC RELATIONS, CT'D

ROLE	DESCRIPTION & QUALIFICATIONS	SPECIFIC RESPONSIBILITIES
Political Educator	Political education is an indispensable recruitment tool, a way to engage with takeover home residents in an ongoing way, and an avenue for leadership identification and development. It also grounds the pragmatic work of takeover in the broader ideological work of the Politics of Love (see Introduction for more). Political educators should be knowledgeable about the history and political rationale of taking over property, as well as the best practices for doing so.	Develop curriculum Lead information sessions Support new members in growing their skills and leadership within the organization
Media Spokesperson	Dealing with the media can be tricky to navigate, in large part because the privacy of residents and crew members is important for their safety. Having a predetermined media strategy can keep the crew from being caught off guard and accidentally divulging too much. A media spokesperson is likely to be part of the core leadership team and should work with the rest of the leadership to map out how engaging with the media can be strategically aligned.	Develop media strategy with core leadership Field all media inquiries and communicate plan for media response/redirection Train others for media engagement as needed

MOVE-IN DAY

ROLE	DESCRIPTION & QUALIFICATIONS	SPECIFIC RESPONSIBILITIES
Move-In Day Shot Caller	On move-in day, decision-making is hierarchical and roles are more concrete than in other day-to-day PPA work. A predetermined shot caller is in charge. This person is typically a more experienced member of the crew who can think on their feet. They should have experience and training with nonviolent civil disobedience, and be willing to take practical and legal responsibility for all move-in day activities.	Run the show on move-in day Make quick decisions when the unexpected happens Communicate with law enforcement, neighbors, media or other arrivals to the scene (if a different point person for these roles has not been assigned)
Mover(s)	Move-in day for takeover homes is the same as a more conventional move-in day in many ways. Movers should be able to carry heavy furniture, household items, and personal belongings and move with confidence.	Obtain and operate moving equipment as needed (truck, dollies, etc.) Carry furniture and belongings into the takeover home
Move-In Day Family Support Person	One person should be the designated point person for guiding the new residents through the move-in day process. The people moving into the house should always know that they are not alone, the crew has their back, and they know the plan to follow if anything goes wrong.	Discuss the plan with the new residents before move-in day Periodically check in with the family during the move Field questions and provide reassurance

A homeless family moves into a takeover house in Northeast Philadelphia in 1996. Photo by Harvey Finkle.

Children embrace each other while living in a KWRU homeless encampment at 4th and Lehigh in Philadelphia in 1995. Photo by Harvey Finkle.

Navigating Fear and Risk

The kind of high-stakes collaboration involved in housing takeovers requires clear communication about, and shared understandings of, potential risks and outcomes. Anyone who engages in housing takeovers assumes risk, but consequences often differ. Tradespeople, government employees, and academics may face professional risk. Crew members who engage in nonviolent civil disobedience by disregarding police orders risk arrest. People with outstanding bench warrants risk escalated legal consequences during police interactions. Furthermore, participants who experience systemic discrimination due to race, class, gender identity, sexual orientation, disability, immigration status, lack of access to legal and financial resources, or other factors typically face more risk from police and the courts. There needs to be more safety planning and potentially more protection built into the process for these people, though risk should never be a barrier to participating in the movement. There is a role in the process for everyone.

Every person who is a part of a Poor People's Army takeover crew is required to have completed a nonviolent civil disobedience training. We offer this training to both organizations and individuals. Additionally, we do not recruit new crew members without having numerous one-on-one meetings and conversations with people already involved. Those conversations include a deep dive into the risks of the process and also explain that there are many different roles with different levels of risks attached. People who are not comfortable going into the house can be in a support role: being there outside the house for the takeover, being a contact person over the phone, raising money to help pay for supplies and storage, calling the press, live-streaming what goes on, and more. These are all less risky roles that matter just as much as roles with higher risk of arrest.

Paradoxically, people who are actually more protected from negative consequences due to their social and financial resources may overestimate the risk of participating in housing takeovers. Those who have not experienced poverty and state violence are more likely to falsely believe, consciously or unconsciously, that police only harass "bad" people. They also may find it easier to focus on what they have to lose, which can make them more reluctant to move in opposition to state systems. Crew members should have frank discussions about how race, class background, and privilege may impact risk tolerance. This helps understand where resistance to risk is coming from while still respecting the boundaries of every crew member. Individuals' risk tolerances are likely to evolve over time, and there will always be places to help in the movement at different levels of risk.

Everyone in the movement may have shared experiences of fear, regardless of their role. Fear may manifest in many ways: as bravado, avoidance/ghosting, and/or promising to do something and then not following through. The best way to work through fear is to have frequent conversations among crew members about boundaries, plan extensively for various outcomes, and depend on each other to have our backs. Fear is metabolized in community, and strong community support within the ranks of a takeover home crew can help provide context and perspective on what the fear may be trying to communicate. Furthermore, political education and a deep shared understanding of the historical moment and the moral stance the crew is taking may root people into their values and bring everyone the strength to do what they feel is right, despite any discomfort that may follow.

CHAPTER 2

Identifying a Target Takeover Home

A crew cannot start housing families in takeover homes if they have not identified viable properties. This chapter will outline how to find, research, and inspect potential homes.

We have attempted to break down this process into as clear a set of steps as possible. It is important to note, however, that housing takeovers are inherently less formal because of the close relationships between crew members, the different needs of each takeover, and the off-the-grid nature of the work.

Finding a Potential Takeover Home

It is possible to find takeover home leads online; the Department of Housing and Urban Development (HUD) lists properties available for sale on their website, hudhomestore.gov. That said, the best way to see what properties might make good takeover homes is to search in person. These location-scouting trips should be carried out in pairs by crew members who live nearby and are familiar with the area. To keep a low profile while scouting, these crew members should drive a car that will look like it belongs in the target neighborhoods. One person should take down addresses and notes while the other drives.

On these initial lead-generating drives, location scouts are responsible for the first-pass screening of a property. They should get a general sense of the condition of the home, its occupancy status, and the demographics of the block. If the house looks vacant and structurally sound from the street, scouts will look around to make sure it seems safe to approach the property; if it does, they will look in the windows to briefly assess the conditions of the floors and walls. They will make sure there are no broken windows, and that there is an electric box present with no lock on it. They will also look for signs that the abandoned home is owned by the government rather than privately owned. In some areas, white sheets covering the windows or paperwork on the windows or front door can be a clue that the property is owned by HUD. If there are any print-outs posted with information about recent inspections, this can also provide clarity about who is maintaining the property and how often. Appendix A contains the checklist that our location scouts use for their first-look inspection.

Over time, identifying a good candidate for a takeover will become second nature and will not require formal dedicated scouting trips.

Cheri Honkala converts a HUD-owned abandoned building into a takeover home in 1989. Photo by Joel Severson.

Poor People's Army crew members frequently notice potential homes during the normal course of our day.

Researching a Property

Once location scouts have identified a potential takeover home, crew members need to access public records to learn more about the property. This information is not uniformly accessible in all areas. Some cities have public-facing online databases, but others may keep the records in city hall. Crew members can try searching "property records [county or city name]" online to find local government databases. It may be necessary to enlist the help of friendly real estate agents or city officials, but we advise serious caution when approaching and feeling out the sympathies of people with ties to the government.

The following questions should be answered in this research process:

- Who owns the property?
- Is it occupied or vacant?
- Is it up for auction?
- Is it a safe property to live in? If not, what would it take to make it safe?
- Who has a personal, financial, or political stake in this property?

Who owns the property? **The tactics in this book are designed for taking over government-owned properties.** Taking over private property would be much more dangerous and less strategic than taking over government-owned property, for several reasons. First, most people believe that government resources, including publicly owned property, should be of use to the public. This belief seeds the ground for understanding our moral stance regarding this project of survival. Second, government agencies are more subject to public opinion than private owners and—at least in theory—could be held to account if they treat takeover home residents with cruelty. Third, properties owned by the Department of Housing and Urban Development are less likely to be monitored and fall under a different legal jurisdiction than privately owned properties.

Is it occupied or vacant? **An ideal takeover home is vacant.** Vacancy can be tricky to establish even if the property has the promising signs of being owned by the government, listed for sale, and having no official residents on record. If someone else is making use of the property in any way, then it is not a good candidate for a takeover house, even if it is not being used by the owner. For example, in some neighborhoods, people will sell drugs out of abandoned homes, which automatically disqualifies those homes from being viable takeover properties. Good signs that a property is truly vacant include flyers and mail stuck in the door, no lights on, no trash cans in the front yard, an empty porch, the absence of window air conditioning units, and grass growing over walkways. One way to check for vacancy is to knock on the door in the early evening; if someone answers, you can avert suspicion by asking for a random person by name and pretending that you knocked on the wrong door.

Is it up for auction? **An ideal takeover home is not up for auction.** Homes that are up for auction have a good chance of already being on a real estate developer's radar. In cases where government agencies are friendly with developers, the public bidding process is probably not as straightforward as it appears. While difficult to prove, we strongly suspect that the main purpose of the "public" bidding process is often to create a legal paper trail for a handshake property transfer agreement. On the other hand, houses that are up for auction may allow the public (including our crew members) to tour the property and better assess its condition. In cases where only up-for-auction properties are available, it can become necessary to take the risk; however, it is important to keep in mind that

A mother and child in their takeover home in 1996. Photo by Harvey Finkle.

the property once again becomes privately-owned if a developer does purchase it.

Is it a safe property to live in? If not, what would it take to make it safe? **A takeover home must be structurally sound.** Takeover home residents deserve safe, solid housing. If a house is falling apart, has broken windows, or has a hole in the roof, it is too expensive to restore to responsible safety conditions. If the roof of the property is not visible from the street, crew members can check satellite photos of the property to get a clearer view. All windows and doors need to be able to securely lock. **A takeover home must have intact electrical wiring.** Wiring that is intact and up to code is necessary for residents to have utilities in their takeover home. The presence of an electrical box outside the window is a good sign. **A takeover home must also have working plumbing.** The takeover home residents will need running water. Because copper pipes are often stolen from vacant properties to be sold, it is important to ensure that the pipes have not been taken. Leaks and missing pipes are usually too expensive to repair or replace. Many of these elements may not be able to be verified until the crew is able to gain entry for further inspection, but it is helpful to keep them in mind from the very beginning.

Who has a personal, financial, or political stake in the property? **An ideal takeover home is in a poor neighborhood.** Wealthy neighbors tend to be considerably more hostile towards takeover home residents and more likely to get politicians or the police involved. By contrast, we have found that many poor neighbors show generosity and find common ground with the new takeover home residents, sometimes even offering food or mattresses. **An ideal takeover home is on a block with similar racial demographics to the residents that will move in.** Takeover home residents are usually safer and more inconspicuous on blocks with neighbors who look like them (see Chapter 5). Also, **an ideal takeover home is not located near politicians' homes or areas of short-term development interest.** The Poor People's Army has found ward leaders, block captains, and city council members to be especially hostile to takeover home residents. While neighbors of a similar class background may be happy that a vacant property is now providing housing, wealthy and powerful neighbors are far more likely to see such properties as ways to make money. The presence of takeover home residents may be perceived as a threat to property values, or frustrate the plans of a political player with schemes for that specific block. A working knowledge of which blocks are politically significant can help reduce the risk of government interference on behalf of developers.

Taking a Closer Look: Inspecting Property Interiors

The final inspections that determine whether a home is suitable for takeover require going inside. Crew members should gain entry to the home with the assistance of a trusted handyperson who can change the locks and give crew members the new keys. A crew member should accompany the handyperson with a clipboard, professional attire, a badge on a lanyard, and a confident demeanor to help lend authority to this process. When deciding who will fill this role, we consider what people in our area would expect a city or real estate official to look like in terms of race, gender, and age. It is also beneficial if they fit the presumed "look" of a contractor or maintenance person as much as possible.

A grandmother and grandchild play in a takeover home in the early 1990s. Photo by Harvey Finkle.

The next step is the assessment by a plumber and an electrician. A crew member, once again dressed professionally and carrying a clipboard, should accompany each of these professionals on a walk-through. The plumber and electrician should evaluate the safety of the home and estimate the cost of repairs. Crew members should test also for lead paint during these walk-throughs using a test kit. These kits are available at most hardware stores as well as online. Crew members should also keep an eye out for other obstacles to living in the house safely and comfortably. Some issues that disqualify the property, such as basement flooding, may only be discovered upon entering the house.

CHAPTER 3

Setting Up Utilities and Services

The Poor People's Army operates under the ethos that takeover home residents deserve the same basic necessities as conventionally-housed people. This chapter outlines the process of connecting a takeover home to utilities and services that are required for daily life.

In an ideal world, turning on utilities and setting up homes for new tenants would be done through official channels. Most of the time, calling the utility company to set up utilities will be the best way to get them turned on. This is most possible when housing takeovers are not on the company's radar and those involved are not already known to local governments. In general, utility companies do not concern themselves with legal rights to the residence.

However, people need safe access to heat, water, and electricity before these official channels can be activated. Extralegal means become required when there is 1) urgency to getting the family in the house (e.g. unavailability of temporary accommodation), 2) government surveillance of utility turn-on requests, or 3) a short time window to move in (for example, if the property is frequently surveilled by government agencies or neighbors). Additionally, in areas where housing takeovers are common and HUD seeks to squash them, houses are often stripped or even sabotaged to prevent takeover, leading to greater difficulties when setting up utility services. This chapter explains some fundamentals about how to get these essentials up and running.

Setting the Stage

Utilities should be set up before someone is living in the house. Two things can help to accomplish this: having the right team and securing an affidavit.

Having a strong team is a bigger priority than anything else for setting up utilities. An electrician and plumber can not only fix problems in a house, but can also help the crew to identify problems that are a barrier to the takeover before it begins. When official channels are not an option for turning on utilities, these experts can sometimes do so themselves safely and quickly. Non-expert involvement and tinkering is *never* recommended, both because of threats to the safety of future residents and because prolonged work can raise suspicion.

A generic affidavit that establishes residency can be useful support. This document can be written by a lawyer or adapted from a template and notarized. In many places, anyone can turn on the utilities without proof of residency, but this is subject to local regulations.

Essential Services

Gas

For safety and ease of setup, the Poor People's Army usually avoids using gas in takeover homes. Sometimes gas is already on, or there is a lock on the meter that can simply be cut off; in these cases, it can sometimes be easiest to continue using it. Otherwise, our experience is that it is much safer to use an electric-top stove and electric heaters than turning on the gas to the house. If setting a house up with gas seems viable, the crew will need a professional willing to undertake that process, and to respond immediately to any smells or leaks. It is crucial to check for gas leaks and fire hazards before moving in.

Water

Water is a vital service to set up, for obvious reasons and reasons that may not be as obvious. When children will be living in a takeover home, we consider a lack of running water to be an unacceptable risk, as this is grounds for Child Protective Services (CPS) involvement. CPS has a history of intentionally targeting poor and homeless families that engage in activism and projects of survival, and we never want to give them an added incentive to criminalize families within our movement. A plumber, or at least someone with substantial plumbing experience, is an essential member of a takeover crew. This is true regardless of whether official channels are used to turn on the water or not.

Turning a house's water supply on and off is a fairly straightforward process. It can, in theory, be undertaken by anyone with the right knowledge and tools. Once a crew member accesses the water meter, which is usually on the ground between the house and the street, they can use a water meter valve key—a long T-shaped piece of metal with a hook on the end—to turn the water on from that position. These can be purchased online, and some plumbers might already have them.

Before turning on the water, crew members should station themselves throughout the home to make sure any leaks are caught immediately. Bathrooms, kitchen sinks, and basements should be monitored for leaks with particular care. One crew member should be in position to shut the water valve off from inside the home in case of flooding. Crew members should turn on all the sinks, flush the toilets a few times, and do a final check that there are no leaks before leaving. If there is a leak, crew members will need to try and get the pipes mended, but this can be so expensive that it often makes the home only viable in the short term, if at all.

Electric

When identifying a house, it can be helpful to find one in which the electrical box is already unlocked. Locked boxes can still be opened, and there are plentiful online resources for removing some of the

*A PPEHRC member repairs a takeover home in the late 1990s.
Photo by Harvey Finkle.*

easier locks, but more complex locking systems may pose a problem. Once the box is unlocked, crew members should attempt to get power connected to the house by contacting the local electric company and putting the electric bill in the new residents' names.

This cannot always be done, however, for various reasons. Before turning anything on, it will help to gather information and make contingency plans around how connecting electricity may trigger a surveillance mechanism and increase risk for that particular takeover home. For example, if the power comes on in a certain house, the electric company is notified and may alert the city. In some cases, a signal is sent to the electric company immediately when the electricity is first turned on. Once a signal is sent that there has been tampering, the electrical company can quickly stop the flow of electricity to the residence and will sometimes even send a technician to physically disconnect the house wires from the pole. An electrician can help to bypass some of these systems. Once the electricity is connected in a takeover home, the electrician will assess the breaker and ensure that the wiring is safe. Sometimes previous people occupying an abandoned property will do unskilled work to turn the power on, and this can lead to dangerous wiring. An electrician will be on the lookout for this, as well as any other safety hazards.

Connecting: Internet and Schools

Internet

Getting internet service right away can be helpful, but is not always necessary to do before move-in. Nonetheless, we recommend it be up and running as soon as possible, so that new residents can have access to resources and entertainment. This helps those first few nerve-wracking days in the takeover home pass more quickly. Later, internet access will be needed to pay bills, communicate with teachers, and access medical help and records. Gaining internet access is becoming easier as better "hotspot" devices can be

Cheri Honkala holds her son Guillermo Santos and joins with members of the Deaf-Blind Committee for Human Rights at the PPEHRC Truth Commission in Ohio in 2006. Photo by Harvey Finkle.

quickly set up without hardwiring a connection. For long-term WiFi setup, however, one ironic silver lining of the corporatization of the internet is that cable companies are much less interested in figuring out the specifics of an individual's or family's circumstances than they are in taking their money. In our experience, cable providers do not ask too many questions about the particulars before setting up cable and internet in a takeover home.

Internet access has become even more essential for kids who are attending school. During COVID lockdowns of 2020, kids needed reliable internet to be able to attend school at all. While there has not been a long-term return to virtual learning for most students, there are still regularly days where schools will move to virtual learning due to weather conditions, COVID surges, or other circumstances. Also, many school assignments require internet access to complete.

School Preparation and Paperwork

Children can be very resilient during the process of moving into a takeover home, but smoothing the way for a normal routine in advance can help them adjust. Being able to attend school as usual is a central point of continuity in that process.

Public school registration usually requires several documents. These may include documents such as:

- The child's birth certificate or a notarized copy
- The child's valid passport
- Baptismal certificate (with date of birth) or a notarized copy
- Notarized statement indicating date of birth
- Prior school records indicating the date of birth
- Proof of address

Given that many families are unable to produce these documents, the crew should proactively establish a relationship with education lawyers in their area so that if there is pushback to enrollment, the education lawyer can contact the school. Once a lawyer is on board, a crew member will write a letter, preferably on the law firm's official letterhead, stating that the child lives in the district and asking that they be allowed to enroll. In our experience, this pushback occurs about one-third of the time. If school officials attempt to bar the child from enrolling, the crew will involve the lawyer, who will contact the school to warn them of the possibility of legal action based on their refusal to register a child in the district.

Setting up a bus stop should also be a part of the school preparation process. This might take a couple of weeks, so someone from the crew should be prepared to give kids a ride to school until a bus stop is secured. Going to school online (or starting school online) can also be an option.

CHAPTER 4

Orienting Takeover Home Residents

This chapter will discuss the intake and orientation process. During this process, crew members meet with people who need housing and prepare them for living in a takeover home. People reach out for housing support for many different reasons, but most of them involve life events that are distressing and isolating. Housing seekers are almost always grappling with additional unmet needs that go beyond shelter. A human and holistic approach to partnering with the person in meeting these needs requires leading with love and listening, while letting politics and logistics come second.

Step 1: Get children set up for the intake

About nine out of ten people who seek housing with the Poor People's Army are single mothers with children. If the person who has reached out for support has children with them, the intake crew member should ask if they would like their children to be present for the intake and defer to their expertise as a parent.

Should the caregiver decide to have the intake conversation in private, their children should be situated safely in another room with other crew members or older children who have been through a similar experience. It can also be the case that older children and teenagers are calmed by having younger children to look after. People doing childcare should follow the child's lead, and should emphasize building a positive relationship with the child and hon-

A child plays with a yo-yo in his takeover home in the mid 1990s.
Photo by Harvey Finkle.

oring their choices rather than putting pressure on them to respond to their situation in a specific way. Kids may want to draw, play a game, sit quietly, talk about how they're feeling, talk about something entirely unrelated, or a combination of these activities, or none of them. Whatever they choose, it is important to have food and drinks available for both children and parents.

Step 2: Meet immediate material needs

Usually, the most pressing concern is where this family will sleep the night of intake. Assuring the person that this most urgent need will be met by any means necessary is an important trust-building step. This may involve tapping one of the resources on the organization's list of non-takeover home housing. It is much easier to talk and strategize about meeting a long-term need for housing when the immediate need for a place to sleep is taken care of. This is another great moment to rely on current and former takeover home residents for both emergency same-day housing and peer support for the new family.

Step 3: Meet immediate emotional needs

With short-term sleeping arrangement worries out of the way, the person will most likely shift to sharing the circumstances that have led to them reaching out for housing support. The role of the intake crew member for this part of the conversation is to attentively listen to their story without judgment. This may be the first time the housing seeker is encountering this kind of support, especially if they have tried to navigate "official" services in the past, so building trust may take time and patience. The circumstances that lead people to become homeless are traumatic, whether it is due to domestic violence, foreclosure, eviction, death of a loved one, or other emergencies. The intake crew member should hold space for how the person is feeling and affirm their right to safe and stable housing for them, their children, and others in their care.

Step 4: Exhaust all personal housing options

This step involves collaborative problem-solving and should not begin until the housing seeker has met their immediate needs for rest, food, and emotional recovery. Once the housing seeker is able to relax and think clearly, the intake crew member can begin to help them explore short- to medium-term solutions for housing. Staying with a crew member or a broader member of the PPA network provides immediate safety, but the process of finding a long-term housing solution often takes considerable time, so a stopgap plan is necessary in between. The best option is to find temporary accommodations with a member of their social network, which secures safety for the person or family while making sure that crew member or supporter space can stay available for the emergency short-term step this person or family is moving out of. A friend, family member, or other community member with room to take them in can provide both emotional and material support. The crew member can support the housing seeker in thinking through all of their social connections and reaching out to ask for help.

Katie Engle, self-proclaimed Lady of Poverty, sits on 7th Street in front of the Philadelphia office of Housing and Urban Development in the early 1990s. Katie was living on 7th street at the time. Photo by Harvey Finkle.

Step 5: Exhaust all government and non-profit social services

If the housing seeker's personal connections cannot give them a place to stay, the next step is to apply for housing through existing programs run by the city or local non-government organizations

(NGOs). It is important to be familiar with what is "officially" available in the local context.

In Philadelphia, where the Poor People's Army is headquartered, the city has an Office of Homeless Services that directs people to call a phone number or visit a physical intake center. There are separate services listed for youth and for people experiencing domestic violence. On numerous occasions, the Poor People's Army has sent a representative to accompany a housing seeker and document the city's official assessment process. What we have found time and again is that the "official" options are often insufficient and unsafe, with waiting lists so long that a family may never actually receive shelter placement. It is common that the city will ask the housing seeker to sign a document absolving the city of responsibility for housing them in exchange for a bus pass to wherever they would like to go next. In the rare instance that a shelter spot is available, some require children and their parents to separate. For those who accept a shelter placement, most people find the conditions to be distressing, dehumanizing, and even dangerous.

Even though they are unlikely to provide the help that the housing seeker truly needs, documenting attempts to move through official channels serves the purpose of demonstrating the political necessity of housing takeovers. It counters the narrative that housing takeovers bypass "better" options provided by the city. Housing seekers may be more politically committed to the crew's vision and ready to occupy a takeover home after crossing off every other option.

Step 6: Explain the takeover home process, responsibilities, and risks

After all other avenues have been ruled out, the intake crew member should work with the housing seeker to determine if they are a good candidate for living in a takeover home. The most important responsibility of takeover home residents is to keep takeover homes free of drugs and violence. If the housing seeker is unable to follow these conditions, they are not a good candidate for a takeover home. This is not to say that the Poor People's Army will not work with them or support them. We partner with a holistic addiction recovery organization here in Philadelphia that requires people receiving services to work with the PPA as part of their recovery. This is born out of the philosophy that one must heal in part by changing the world that made them sick, as systemic political and economic forces play a role in addiction. We firmly believe in not demonizing people with addiction, and only refer people in our networks to our partners who also see homeless people as human beings instead of objects of pity or problems to be solved. Because of the risks associated with living in a takeover home and the likelihood of police or government involvement, however, the PPA will not knowingly house someone in active addiction in a takeover home. This is a no-exceptions policy that we have developed as a way to protect the entire group of current takeover home residents.

When it comes to violence in takeover homes, we are usually referring to domestic violence. The PPA does not believe in criminalizing people who have been abusive, and believes that incarceration continues cycles of violence rather than breaking them. To protect the safety of everyone housed in takeover homes, however, as well as to best support the person experiencing abuse, we have required people who have engaged in violent behavior to leave takeover homes before. Alternatives-to-violence programs are better equipped to help people break cycles of abuse than we are.

The risk of scrutiny and persecution from government agencies, politicians, police, and neighbors applies to residents as people and also their belongings. The Poor People's Army has places to keep residents' most sacred belongings safe—a roster of free or cheap storage locations exists alongside a roster of potential takeover homes, and many of PPA's funds are spent on storage—but the funding for storage is not always available.

The takeover home residents' responsibilities are spelled out in a

Members of PPEHRC withstand police surveillance as they march with their children for housing, food, and healthcare in Kentucky in 2006. Photo by Harvey Finkle.

Memorandum of Understanding that takeover home residents sign before moving in. (See Appendix B for the full text of the Memorandum of Understanding that we use.)

Step 7: Welcome takeover home residents into the fight for economic human rights

Current and former takeover home residents are uniquely qualified to fight for better conditions for poor and homeless people in the United States. The movement for housing as a human right is led by and for the people most affected; this is a core tenet of the Poor People's Army, and the Memorandum of Understand includes an agreement about participating in the movement.

As previously mentioned, takeover home occupants can pay it forward by offering their space to people with nowhere to sleep, but there are also many other ways to lend one's skills to a movement. This can look like:

- Attending organizing meetings
- Distributing food out of the takeover home or picking up food donations
- Joining sit-ins
- Starting/guiding housing takeovers in other cities
- Leading demonstrations and speaking out
- Providing childcare for others in the movement
- Sharing their experiences and educating others
- Providing temporary housing for others in need
- Joining the housing takeover crew
- Marching in protest
- And many more!

While "movement participation" is in many ways an accurate description of the ways takeover home residents become active in the PPA, it is also something of an oversimplification. The PPA is made up of individuals who have knit our lives together to help each other to survive, and who also engage in both collective analysis of the forces that have pushed us to the margins and collective struggle against those forces. Those relationships and that sense of community originating from shared experience are at the heart of our work. In understanding takeover home residents' political activation and participation, we think of it less as joining a movement and more as becoming an organized participant in a movement those residents are already in.

CHAPTER 5

Moving In, Staying In

This chapter will cover the essentials of not only getting residents set up in their takeover home, but also what will enable them to stay there once they move in.

Planning for Move-In Day

Moving into a takeover home can be a scary process for anyone involved, so organization and planning are important. Everyone who will be there should know exactly what their role is, what to expect, and how to handle any surprise visits from authorities or the media.

The first planning step is to choose a shot caller. This is the person who will be in charge on move-in day. The shot caller is typically a more experienced member of the crew who can think on their feet and is able to communicate effectively with the police, media, and neighbors if need be. They should have experience and training with nonviolent civil disobedience, and be willing to take responsibility for all move-in day activities.

In addition to the shot caller, moving in new residents usually takes about six crew members who can help with moving furniture and belongings. The team will need a car or moving truck to transport any furniture and other household items to the new home, as well as moving equipment like dollies. Sourcing this help and equipment is part of the preparations.

One person should be in charge of supporting the new residents through the move-in process. This person may also be part of the moving crew, but they will periodically check in with the residents and reassure them as needed. The people moving into the house should always know that they are not alone, that the crew has their back, and that everyone understands the plan to follow if anything goes wrong.

A media spokesperson should be assigned in case reporters come to the home during move-in. The Poor People's Army has found this to be much less common in recent years, but it is still good to be prepared. The shot caller may double as the media spokesperson if a crew does not have enough people to fill both roles.

The family that is moving into the home needs to have a cell phone. If nobody in the family has one, the takeover home crew should arrange to get one for them before move-in day. This is essential in case authorities appear at the house and the new residents need support.

The final decision to make during the planning stage is to decide who, if anyone, will participate in arrestable nonviolent civil disobedience if police come to the scene. Housing takeovers are a project of survival first and foremost; they take on a secondary function of political protest only if our hand is forced by the state. Being arrested while others live-stream is a strategic option that can build longer-term safety by calling attention to the state's violent approach towards poor and homeless people. However, it carries a higher level of risk than some other takeover home activities. Those who may be arrested should plan to bring necessary items for jail with them to the takeover: IDs, medication, water, and warm layers. Crew members who may be arrested for the first time should receive detailed information on the experience from those who have gone through it; the process will vary by jurisdiction and depending on the charges, so everyone should have a thorough understanding of what is most likely to happen in their local context after they are taken into custody.

Moving In

It may be tempting to move into a takeover home when it is dark or there aren't many people around. In reality, though, this is more likely to attract unwanted attention because it is out of the ordinary. It is best to move in the whole household in broad daylight, so it looks like anyone else moving into any normal home.

We in the Poor People's Army do our best to keep a stock of donated furniture and household items in storage so that takeover home residents will have everything they need to be comfortable. Window AC units, space heaters, and kitchen appliances are hot-ticket items that we try to provide, along with a supply of groceries and

A family moves into a takeover home in the late 1990s. Photo by Harvey Finkle.

food. The moving crew may need to provide furniture assembly and window AC installation on move-in day so that the new residents have everything they need when the crew leaves. Rugs, lamps, wall art, and other furnishings will make the property look and feel like a home. Some families may want to display family photos, but many choose to keep these most precious personal items secure in one of our storage units for safekeeping. Movers should also hang opaque curtains, sheets, or paper over the windows to provide privacy for the new residents.

Another key part of the move-in process is bringing and posting signs inside and outside the home. Inside the house, movers should hang a sign with emergency contact info for a support contact from the takeover home team, usually someone from leadership who can help them with any hiccups. Movers should also

Cheri Honkala posts signs in a new takeover home in 2021. Photo by Matt Pillischer.

put up protest signs inside that make it clear that the takeover is a political statement and that the residents have organizational and community support. These should be visible inside the house, in case police or inspectors enter and try to evict the residents. Outside the house, the moving crew should post signs on the door that alert visitors if there are children, Autistic people, Deaf people, or someone with another disability in the house. This is to protect the residents against violence from police or other people trying to remove them from the house.

Most people naturally embrace and want to help others, especially neighbors in poor neighborhoods. Sometimes, however, a politically-motivated block captain will notice the takeover in progress and call police down to the home. When the Poor People's Army first began taking over homes in the early 1990s, this would happen at about one out of every seven takeovers; it is much less common now because we have a better understanding of which blocks and neighborhoods have residents with political connections. If police or media show up during move-in, crew members other than the shot caller or media spokesperson should not answer them except to say that they need to consult with their team. The shot caller will handle any police communication, and the media spokesperson will handle any media communication.

Police Disruption and Arrestable Resistance

The Poor People's Army protocol for police presence almost always involves pivoting to nonviolent resistance and live-streaming police action on social media. This approach takes advantage of the opportunity to publicize the humanitarian work of taking over homes and the cruelty of the state's response. For this reason, we choose to act as though all of the crew is willing to stand their ground and be arrested, although in reality some people have decided in advance to comply with police instructions before the situation comes to the point of arrest. The longer we can draw out the interaction, the longer we have for supporters, the media, or other witnesses to arrive, and for members of the crew to attract a larger audience to the live stream.

A police officer removes Cheri Honkala from her first takeover home on 38th Ave in Minneapolis in the late 1980s. Photo by Joel Severson.

As soon as authorities arrive, the crew should immediately huddle up. Politely telling authorities, "Excuse us for a second" often works to give the crew a minute to plan. In the huddle, the shot caller maps out the strategy for the rest of the encounter.

To send the message that the crew will not leave voluntarily, the shot caller will choose a place inside the home for everyone to take a seat as a group. Crew members who have decided in advance to be arrested should position themselves next to someone who they are prepared to be with for the next 24 to 72 hours. The shot caller should be furthest from the front of the group so that they are last to be arrested, allowing them to keep an eye on the delegation who are being taken into custody. Because the shot caller also tends to have the most experience, they will often be next to the member of the group who might need the most support during the detention. Those who plan to be arrested should pass valuables to others who are not going to be arrested for safekeeping and write the phone number of a designated jail support crew member on their body in ink that will not rub off.

At this point, the police will continue instructing the crew to disperse. They may give three warnings before making arrests–this is the legal standard the police are bound to follow, although this does not always happen. After the second warning, the shot caller will direct anyone who is not prepared to get arrested to go outside and join any onlookers who may have assembled.

For the people who do get arrested, it usually happens one by one. By the time arrests are imminent, the expectation is that the crew will comply with all police instructions during the arrest process. We do not recommend waiting and forcing the police to carry people out. History suggests this will prompt a higher charge and often escalates the situation, increasing the risk of police brutality. Antagonizing authorities unnecessarily is counter to the strategy of our housing takeovers.

Staying in the Home

If the move-in is not thwarted by police intervention, the new residents can begin settling in and learning to live in the takeover home. Once the adrenaline of the move starts to subside, new residents will likely experience emotions that have been put on hold. A compassionate ear should be there to continue reassuring the residents that they are supported and their grief is an appropriate response to the injustice and violence they have experienced.

For the first several days after a family moves in, we organize a watch list of people who take shifts keeping an eye on the home to support the family and keep them safe. If the family is nervous and would benefit from a crew member's presence, the PPA family support person can keep them company inside the home. Then, once the family becomes more comfortable, the support person can keep watch from a vehicle parked outside to monitor comings and goings.

Once new residents are settled into the takeover home, the goal is to keep them comfortable in the home for as long as possible. The typical length of stay is about nine months. In Philadelphia, the longest stay has been three years, and the shortest was about two hours. Moving people repeatedly is dangerous, time-consuming, and costly, so it is best for them to stay in a takeover home as long as they can. There are a number of factors that can support residents in achieving this goal.

Cheri Honkala finishes her shift on house watch to protect families in a takeover home in the late 1980s. Photo by Joel Severson.

Staying on good terms with neighbors

Relationships with neighbors can be tricky to navigate, and will be highly context-dependent. From the moment that the team arrives at the property, all should be mindful that they will be under surveillance not just from state authorities, but also from those next door. The more that can be done to make neighbors happy, the better. This includes things such as:

- Mowing the lawn
- Repairing aesthetic damage to the home's exterior
- Applying a fresh coat of paint
- Picking up trash on the curb and sidewalk
- Following rules for trash pickup and appropriately disposing of any garbage that is not picked up elsewhere
- Keeping music volume down
- Avoiding drugs, alcohol, and violence

There may also be unspoken social customs that differ from block to block. For example, some neighborhoods may frown on smoking cigarettes on the front porch, and takeover home residents can be counseled to remain discreet by taking a walk to smoke instead. This is why it is crucial that the housing takeover is led by people working in their own community who know the area well.

When neighbors are open to establishing a relationship with new residents, this is a key asset. Approaching with consideration and caution is key as a first step, but can lead to deeper relationships with the family in the long-run. The PPA has had several experiences in which neighbors have come out to support the family, and even played a role in getting cops or authorities to leave. Such alliances are best established when the team and the family show the utmost respect to the property.

Weathering harassment from authorities

Over our thirty years of housing people in takeover homes, the Poor People's Army has gained extensive familiarity both with eviction law and with the ways police regularly violate that law with little to no consequences. Technically, eviction must involve a civil court process, but police sometimes try other tactics to force families out of takeover homes. This usually happens within the first few days or weeks. Police may intimidate the family or destroy their belongings. In rare circumstances, the Poor People's Army has witnessed more extreme examples. For example, at a takeover house in 1998 the police sent a bomb squad, claiming that there was a bomb in a refrigerator. In another instance, a police officer put his foot through the door of a takeover home. Families moving into takeover homes are always made aware of this risk: that police can decide to appoint themselves judge and jury at any point, and that, as we often say, "Rights are only in the movies." We reassure them, however, that we have years of experience running these processes and have built up our own legal tactics to fight unlawful evictions and protect their right to housing.

Police are not the only type of authority that may try to force families out of takeover homes. The Department of Housing and Urban Development or the Sheriff's department will more often come check on houses that they expect may be the target of a future takeover. Licensing and Inspections has been known to enter a property while takeover home residents are out and cut wires, then return to the property later and claim that, because the wires are cut, the property must be condemned and residents must vacate.

Government representatives have repeatedly shut off the water supply to a takeover house from the street when other harassment campaigns failed. The Poor People's Army's strategy to fend off their intervention is to establish a rotating water patrol of supporters to park their cars on top of the water shutoff access point. Resistance can be creative and should remain de-escalatory and nonviolent to lower the risk of retaliation and best protect all crew members and families living in takeover homes.

Another tactic that we have experienced is outright bribery. A purported "owner" of an abandoned house once showed up with cash to try to coax a family out of it.

In all of these instances, the protocol for the takeover home residents is the same: do not engage and call their emergency contact from the takeover home crew. The shot caller or another crew leader should be the only person to speak to the would-be evic-

Children play with dolls in a takeover home in 2020. Photo by Matt Pillischer.

tor. There is no substitute for experience in this case; depending on which agency is on the premises, the rhetoric and handling of the situation could vary from asserting the family's rights to a civil court process to yielding to their demands and promising to come help the family move out.

De-escalation approaches vary based on the shot caller's experience, identities, and instincts. We have found that, for conversations like this, a matter-of-fact and official tone tends to be the most successful way of meeting our goals for the conversation: to convince the agitator to stop pursuing eviction, or at least buy time to fight the process in the longer term rather than the immediate moment. The emergency contact from the crew will introduce themself over the phone and explain the following to the aggressor:

- An eviction like this is out of the jurisdiction of local police.
- The eviction belongs in the jurisdiction of federal marshals because this is government property. At minimum, it should go to civil court.
- This is not a matter that the police can just handle on the spot; the family that is residing in the property has a right to be there.

The underlying message is always the same: "We have this under control, we are responsible, and we know what we are doing." The PPA has found it more successful in these emergency situations to avoid speaking ideologically or politically, and to instead focus on projecting confidence, certainty, and expertise in housing processes. If de-escalation does not work, the next steps are immediate and twofold: one crew leader should drive to the house right away to start recording what the police are doing, and another should get a lawyer on the phone. The person recording can also call media contacts to the scene as a way to put additional pressure on the police, though the crew member's recording is the priority. The crew member speaking to the lawyer will ask them to file an injunction against the eviction (an injunction is a civil filing that makes note of an unlawful occurrence; we will discuss this more in Chapter 6). In the majority of situations, however, assertively invoking procedure and hierarchy will be successful in backing the agitator down.

If there ever comes a point when the safety of the takeover home residents is in question, the crew should find another place for them immediately. The wellbeing of takeover home residents takes precedence over all other considerations and must be protected.

Communication and community

Staying in active contact with the Poor People's Army is mandatory for all families in takeover homes, regardless of how long they have been living there. We need them to stay engaged with our leadership and community because there is always a risk of agitation or harassment. Each family's safety is interconnected with the safety of all takeover home residents and consistent communication is non-negotiable.

Beyond safety concerns, families also benefit immensely from the care and belonging that comes from being involved with the PPA. Homelessness can be extremely isolating in and of itself, and the stigma it carries makes it even harder to form social relationships. This is true for both adults and children, who tend to keep their home situation a secret and avoid inviting friends over or sharing much about their lives with peers at school. This makes the peer group of other homeless children, and specifically other children currently living in takeover homes, particularly valuable and supportive. Residents who work with the PPA are not just living in a takeover home; they help with food distribution, attend or run political education sessions, riding buses to demonstrations, and even forming knitting circles with people who are also in takeover homes. Community members' shared housing situations are not often discussed directly, but that shared understanding and experience is instrumental in drawing people together. The PPA is sure to provide gifts for children at holidays and help throw birthday parties in takeover homes, often supporting parents in planning and getting supplies. People don't just deserve a safe roof over their head; they also deserve joy, celebration, and connection.

CHAPTER 6

Sustainability, Advocacy, and Movement Building

Chapters 1 through 5 of this book provide a thorough grounding in how to complete the takeover of one home. Creating a housing takeover *movement*, though, requires more skills, infrastructure, and relationships over time. This chapter will explore the considerations that arise not just in starting a housing takeover movement, but in sustaining one.

Finding a Fiscal Sponsor and Dealing with Nonprofits

The Poor People's Army is not registered with the federal government as a tax-exempt 501(c)(3) nonprofit. Instead, we have a fiscal sponsor who does have that status and supports our work, in addition to supporting the work of other organizations that align with their values that we are not necessarily affiliated with. For other organizations and groups of people interested in housing takeovers, this may be a valuable model to consider.

Fiscal sponsors can provide a variety of services. Donations made to a fiscal sponsor are tax-deductible, which supporters of the work who itemize their taxes may value. This also allows for the disbursement of grants that are only available to 501(c)(3)s, such as those from donor advised funds or larger foundations. Another valuable feature of fiscal sponsors is their pre-existing financial infrastructure. This infrastructure includes donation processing, financial attorneys, bookkeepers, and tax support.

Once a crew or grassroots organization secures fiscal sponsorship, the fiscal sponsor begins accepting donations on their behalf and then transfers those donations to the people on the ground. Most fiscal sponsors take a percentage of donations to help support their operations, so a balance of donations through a fiscal sponsor and direct donations/mutual aid to the crew themselves is ideal.

A fiscal sponsor provides legitimacy that enables an influx of funds from individuals who care about tax-exempt status (and who are often wealthier) as well as more entrenched, better-resourced philanthropic organizations. Unsurprisingly, however, access to these resources does not come without cost or without risk—both for the housing takeover crew and for the fiscal sponsor itself.

501(c)(3)s have embedded themselves in the system that housing takeovers, by necessity, happen outside of. If a nonprofit's support for extralegal housing becomes publicized, it could jeopardize the nonprofit's ability to function within the broader philanthropic landscape.

For the housing takeover crew, the risks are both material and ideological. Working with a fiscal sponsor can create more scrutiny of a housing takeover process, which could possibly increase legal or political risk. Furthermore, we must keep in mind that taking over houses is necessary work precisely because government and government-supported organizations (like nonprofits) fail to actually address the needs of poor people. Taking over houses will never be accepted by the system until we build a new system, at which point taking over houses will no longer be needed. If a fiscal sponsor is pressuring a housing takeover crew to make their work more palatable or less threatening to the status quo, that is not a sign that the housing crew needs to change what they are doing—it is a sign that the fiscal sponsor is not a good fit. As Audre Lorde once said, "The master's tools will never dismantle the master's house."

The Poor People's Army found a fiscal sponsor that was a good fit for us by witnessing that organization's work with both anti-military organizing and global peasant movement organizing. We believed that their work supporting movements that had long been political targets of the United States meant that they would have the experience and analysis needed to work with us without pressuring us to compromise our principles.

Working with Lawyers and the Court System

A successful takeover home crew will need to be prepared to navigate the legal system in a wide variety of ways. Some of this work will require building strong relationships with politically aligned legal professionals; all of this work will require the crew to begin to build their own legal expertise for themselves.

Finding a lawyer

In all probability, a housing takeover crew will need strong working relationships with more than one lawyer because of the highly specialized nature of practicing law. Any lawyer the crew works with will need to share the crew's values and politics enough to be willing to take on the risk of representing a group of people who pose such a significant threat to a city's or county's economic interests. Building trust with these lawyers will be essential.

Finding a lawyer willing and able to take on this level of risk may not be easy. While obtaining pro bono legal support from progressive lawyers was not so difficult in the past, increasing levels of collaboration between law firms and powerful economic institutions like utility providers has significantly increased the number of lawyers barred from using their pro bono time to support the Poor People's Army. Furthermore, there are a number of lawyers from various backgrounds who may be interested in using a high-profile case (such as one connected to a housing takeover) to support their personal ambitions, but are not committed to long-term work and are not invested in our movement.

These challenges when it comes to obtaining legal representation are many, but not insurmountable. We have worked with a variety of lawyers over the years. Many of these lawyers do not specialize in housing law, but are instead using their free time to put their values into practice. Our crew members who have learned the ins and outs of housing law from their time in the movement are often the ones best positioned to bring those lawyers up to speed, and most are able to learn as they go. We have found that sometimes private lawyers are more willing to work for free than public interest lawyers, because of the entanglements between public institutions and economic hegemony.

What can lawyers do?

Lawyers can support housing takeovers in many ways—from helping families obtain affidavits that affirm proof of residency in a takeover home to giving legal advice on writing a book—but the main way lawyers can support our movement is by facilitating dealings with the court system. This happens one of two ways: reactively or proactively. A lawyer can *reactively* help by supporting crew members who have been taken to court or arrested. On the other side of the coin, a lawyer can *proactively* help crew members by taking institutions to court and as a strategy to publicize the injustices of the housing system.

Also on the reactive side, lawyers can sometimes act as on-site legal observers when a crew is expecting police interference with a housing takeover in order to defend against or slow evictions and arrests. Crew members should still defer to the shot caller in such situations, not the lawyer.

Lawyers can also defend crew members against criminal charges in court. One lawyer will usually be able to represent the entire crew as a collective. They will help the crew make their case to the judge, and share any relevant documentation. Lawyers can also help families deal with legal harassment, especially if families are being threatened with the loss of custody of their children. This is one of the most important ways lawyers can help the movement, because it is one of the biggest threats the city has in its arsenal to silence homeless organizers.

On the proactive side, a lawyer can be a powerful asset to help the crew strategize how to best handle any legal situations that arise. As we have stated, the existence of a law is in no way a guarantee that the police and the city interests they represent will adhere to that law. This is especially relevant for laws around illegal evictions from takeover homes, but it applies to other situations as well. Having a lawyer who can sue, or threaten to sue, the police department and the city for breaking eviction law may help deter some severe forms of police and city interference and evictions. We believe that a fear of being sued is the main reason the Philadelphia police do not carry out illegal evictions of families from takeover homes or destroy their belongings as often as they used to. As we mentioned in Chapter 3, lawyers can also respond to school officials who refuse to enroll a child in school on the grounds of their residence in a takeover home. A good lawyer who is prepared and committed to fight for a takeover crew and for families is not a guarantee that people in power won't target us, but it is certainly a valuable asset.

Injunctions are another key legal mechanism that we can use to our advantage. An injunction is a formal declaration filed with the city that unlawful activity is happening, which requires the offending party to halt their actions until they respond through official legal channels. Anyone can start the process of filing an injunction, whether they have a law degree or not. The process typically costs $60-$100, however, which can be prohibitive. We use this strategy most often, when we can afford it, to buy time and create disincentives around illegal evictions and foreclosures. The process of

Cheri Honkala and her son Mark Webber sit beside Meridel Le Sueur in the 1980s. Le Sueur was an iconic activist who took over houses during the Great Depression and was a prolific contributor to the proletarian literature movement. Up and Out of Poverty Now won the right to the pictured property after taking over hundreds of abandoned houses in the Twin Cities. Photo by Joel Severson.

filing an injunction looks different in different cities, but often the first step is to go to city hall and share the intention to file an injunction based on an illegal eviction. City officials will ask the person filing if they have legal representation, which adds useful legitimacy. That said, legal representation is not required, especially for crew members with significant legal experience. The next step of the injunction process simply consists of filling out the paperwork. In the time that an injunction buys, we are able to mobilize our own lawyers, the press, and the power of our communities, to create negative publicity for the aggressor and stop the eviction or foreclosure from happening at all.

Using lawyers and the courts has also been a central element of the

Poor People's Army's longer-term movement strategy. We brought a lawsuit against the government for neglecting its responsibility to house people. While the case was thrown out, the judge who dismissed it did so in a way that provided significant key information to the movement and our lawyers on how best to proceed in bringing the suit again. Lawyers can be a useful partner in spreading the housing takeover movement's main message: that the government is violating homeless people's right to housing, and that they cannot continue to do this without consequences.

Dealing with the Media and Creating Our Own Publicity

Media coverage around takeover homes is complicated for a multitude of reasons. While public opinion can be an asset when wielded against oppressive power, reporters frequently fail to sufficiently prioritize the safety and humanity of the families living in takeover homes. The media and the police work closely together as well, to the point where journalists often arrive on the scene of a housing takeover alongside the police.

Many journalists also reinforce harmful stereotypes about poor people and those living in takeover homes by engaging in caricature and presenting a romanticized narrative of our struggle. When we refuse to uphold mainstream myths about poverty, we are met with media blackouts. Several members of our movement have experienced a cycle of 1) tokenism and heroization, whereupon 2) their refusal to be co-opted or participate in the co-optation of our movement leads to 3) controversy, followed by 4) loss of platform and visibility.

For these reasons, our media strategy is usually to limit contact between official media outlets and takeover home residents and processes as much as possible. That said, we strongly recommend that crew members themselves document any attempts by the state to extralegally intervene in the lives and housing of takeover home residents. Sharing this documentation with the public can also work in our favor and buy us time to mount a more robust defense. This is especially true when it comes from homeless people and/or takeover home crews creating and using that publicity on our own terms. For example, we took over an abandoned church for housing right before Christmas—a high-profile takeover that was successful, in part, because the church and city officials did not want negative publicity that would come from evicting families from a church right before Christmas.

Shining a light on our repression can be a protective response to threats of harm from the state. Our movement has led us to establish multiple tent encampments (commonly referred to as tent cities) in prominent locations, or to turn pre-existing encampments into sites of political protest as a way to refuse the disappearing of poor and homeless people in the United States. This is a powerful strategy that shows the nation and the world that we refuse to suffer in silence. Because our visibility threatens the status quo, it often leads to retaliation from politicians, police, and other state officials. Our best defense against this retaliation is often documenting and continuing to publicize what we are experiencing.

In one instance, city employees and nonprofit workers came to a tent city where mothers and children were protesting together. These agents threatened to take the children into state custody if the families continued to speak up. Other encampment residents used their phones to livestream the agents' actions to a wide online audience, ensuring that if they made good on their threats, their personal complicity would be public. This defense successfully resulted in the case workers backing down and enabled the families

Cheri Honkala and other KWRU/PPEHRC members protest welfare cuts in front of Congress in Washington, D.C. in 1999. Photo by Harvey Finkle.

in the tent city to continue protesting without fear of family criminalization and separation.

Documentation can stop the state from taking illegal or immoral action in the moment, and it can also be used to protect people in court if they are facing trumped-up or escalated charges. Everyone involved in housing takeovers, from crew members to residents, should be knowledgeable about phone security (especially around location services and Face ID), but having a phone available to record and document any riskier situations can be beneficial both in the moment and afterwards.

While publicity can be a helpful tool, there is also a strong need to keep the lives and personal information of takeover home residents as protected from the media as possible. Residents should always be able to choose what, when, and how they share personal information, and crew members should make sure they are preparing residents for the breadth of risks that can come with publicity, especially when it comes to making political statements about housing and homelessness.

Besides having community members document abuses of power and using the media as a tool to shape public opinion and public relations, as we have mentioned in earlier chapters, it is also helpful to have someone prepared to deal with the media if they do show up during a housing takeover. This is especially worthwhile in a situation where the media and the cops show up together. If people are going to be arrested, crew members should create press and documentation as possible to help get information out about the arrests and the extralegal police intervention.

Staying in it for the Long Haul

Long-term involvement in housing takeover work is difficult. Fear, burnout, and overwhelm are common, and are reasonable responses rather than personal failings. Members of our movement have had to come up with a variety of strategies to keep ourselves grounded and motivated—both individually and as a community. We have referenced these strategies in other chapters because they are a throughline that animates our work, but this section will be an opportunity to explore them in detail.

Open communication, strong relationships and community between crew members, and clear boundaries are all essential for sustaining this work in the long term. Before any of those cornerstones can be built, however, every individual in this movement must start with self-awareness and a consistent practice of checking in with themselves. Why are we doing this? What parts of it give us energy? What parts of our lives outside of the movement make us feel good, and how can we make time for them even in small ways? In asking these questions, we return to the Politics of Love—not a romanticized or easy-breezy feeling, but a deep commitment to caring and fighting for ourselves and each other. Centering that love is not always easy, but these reminders of it help us keep going: to know that we care about the people we are engaged in this work with, that we refuse to give up in the face of injustice and exploitation, and that we are fighting back instead.

There are other emotions or states of mind that help us keep going as well. For many members of our movement, humor and silliness are vital—bad puns, over-the-top what-ifs, and whatever else can keep us smiling and laughing. This can also help crew members bond with each other. While the work we are doing is serious, we are not required to be serious all the time to carry it out. We make each other laugh, and we make ourselves laugh as much as we can.

Faith can be another important tool for members of our movement. This does not inherently mean faith in religion, though it certainly can. It can mean faith in our crew members, faith that what we are doing is morally right, and faith that we are building a better alternative to what exists for our communities right now. Creating concrete reminders of that faith—a necklace, a quote written on the wall, a motto, or a song—can make it easier to access in difficult moments as well.

Boundaries and Communication

As we mentioned above, discomfort and fear will always be part of this work, and crew members should never expect them to vanish entirely. Rather, navigating discomfort and fear in ways that maintain our psychological safety and self-determination can feed our souls by bringing us into deep alignment with our values. A commitment to the values of nonviolence and universal human thriving requires that we be diligent not to let ourselves become collateral damage, either at the hands of the oppressive systems we face or at our own hands as we resist those systems. Knowing and asserting our boundaries is essential to this project of survival, based on the premise that everyone deserves to have their needs met. This includes takeover home residents and crew members—and those who are both, as is often the case. In order to continue in the movement for the long term, everyone involved must tend to both their own needs and the needs of others.

What are our boundaries?

Negotiating healthy boundaries can be a useful tool for naming our own needs and understanding those of our collaborators. According to Brené Brown, "Setting boundaries is making clear what's okay and what's not okay, and why." The difference between a dislike and a boundary can be difficult to define, and requires us to engage in a regular process of checking in with ourselves and asking: "Do I not like this, or is it unacceptable and unsustainable to me?" In this work, that means crew members should spend time understanding what they are able to contribute long-term without compromising their own well-being. Everyone's boundaries are different and are likely to evolve over time.

How do we state our boundaries?

The following are examples of boundary statements:

- "Getting arrested is not okay with me."
- "Sundays are my day for personal reflection and rest. I will not engage in any housing takeovers on Sundays."
- "Please don't tell anyone that I'm involved in housing takeovers."
- "This request is making me uncomfortable; can we please revisit this after I've had a chance to think about why that is?"
- "Let's use Signal to discuss this, rather than email or text."
- "I can't commit more than X hours per month."
- "Heavy lifting isn't safe for my back."
- "I can't pay for the storage unit this month."

Understanding one's own boundaries and being able to express them are different skills. Crew members may struggle to communicate boundaries due to conflict avoidance, which is often based in the fear that conflict may threaten their sense of belonging and community. Some may also find themselves swayed by strong personalities or fall into people-pleasing patterns. Crew members may also experience shame around their own boundaries, or judgment about someone else's. All crew members have a moral and strategic responsibility to respect and uphold both our own and our collaborators' boundaries. Strong and clearly communicated boundaries are a key difference between a movement that fizzles out and a movement that lasts.

To mitigate these barriers to boundary-setting, new people should be taught clearly that this is a space where boundaries are strategic in ongoing, collaborative relationships. Established crew members should model the kind of communication they hope to instill in newer crew members. All crew members should know, and remind each other, that there is no expectation of perfection around boundary-setting, but that there is always room to open or re-open boundary conversations and continue the practice of being vulnerable with each other. Communicating our individual limits shows our collaborators that we trust them with our true and tender needs and that we are invested in staying well and staying in this fight beyond this moment.

How do we know when we need a boundary?

Collaborators can help each other explore the effectiveness of their current boundaries by noting how their bodies feel, what makes their energy feel replenished or drained, and what their fellow community members observe about their moods as situations evolve. A common sign that someone may be overstepping their

Cheri Honkala, her son Mark Webber, and other KWRU/PPEHRC members share a smile with author Willie Baptist at the Alternative Convention in Philadelphia in 2000. Photo by Harvey Finkle.

own boundary is a disproportionate need for praise and acknowledgment. Sustained anxiety, interrupted sleep, and an obsessive fixation on a particular risk or scenario can also be warning signs to take a closer look at one's boundaries.

Political Education and Community

The Poor People's Army has been able to keep going for as long as we have because of our sense of shared need. People join our movement because they don't have what they need—housing, food, clothes, baby formula, and so on. From the moment someone connects with us, we see them not as a charity recipient, but rather as someone we are organizing with and who is organizing with us. When a takeover home resident signs their Memorandum of Understanding, they commit to movement participation through

PPA and community members, including Sister Margaret McKenna, Pastor Dave Reppert, and Pastor Keith Collins, take over the Philadelphia Central Library in 2019. Photo by Matt Pillischer.

both education and action. Political education introduces the second axis of shared need, beyond the material: a need to be in relationship with other people who share our lived experience and political consciousness.

Political education is vital to our movement as both a strategic tool and a tool that enables self-love. Understanding the ways that systems of profit work to oppress poor and homeless people is a necessary first step towards unlearning the idea that poverty and homelessness are personal failings. Once members understand this, they are both able to break cycles of shame and self-blame and become best positioned to struggle against these systems. Doing that unlearning and consciousness-building with other poor people fulfills another human need, less tangible but no less powerful: the need for community, belonging, and understanding. While conflict certainly still happens, this shared necessity is the bedrock of our movement, and keeps our relationships strong despite the many challenges we face. For more information about the specifics of our political education work, visit our website at www.poorpeoplesarmy.org.

Poverty and homelessness are deliberately isolating experiences. Community is at the core of our movements for everyone, from the most recently housed takeover home resident to the crew member who has been in the movement for decades. This mutually beneficial community is what makes us different from a charity or nonprofit, and also what gives us the structure we need to take action. While we have laid out our methods in as clear a step-by-step way as possible, we share them knowing that relationships are what makes this work possible, not hierarchies or formal structures. When organizing this far outside of the system, the ground underneath us is always shifting. We offer what has worked for us in the hopes that it will be helpful to other crews and people on the bottom in other cities without overriding their place-based creativity and expertise. What has worked for us most of all is showing up for ourselves, showing up for each other, showing up for our vision of a world where everyone has what they need—and because of our deep interdependence and shared struggle, we know that when we do one of these things, we do all three.

APPENDIX A

Takeover Home Location Scouting Checklists

First-look Checklist

- The property appears vacant.
- No structural issues are visible from the street.
- There is an electric box present and it does not have a lock on it.
- There are no broken windows.
- The inside looks structurally sound, especially floors.
- There is evidence that the property is government owned: white sheets covering the windows and/or paperwork on the front door.

Interior Safety Inspection Checklist

- A plumber has verified that the pipes are present and there are no leaks when turning on faucets.
- An electrician has verified that the wiring is intact and up to code.
- Crew members have conducted a lead paint test.
- Crew members have ruled out structural issues and basement flooding.

APPENDIX B

Takeover Home Resident Memorandum of Understanding

Soldier Takeover Memorandum of Understanding

between Poor People's Economic Human Rights Campaign / Poor People's Army ("PPEHRC") and

_____
(Name)

_____
(Date)

I. Memorandum of Understanding ("Agreement")

This agreement includes information about _____
_____
_____

The reason for this agreement is to ensure _____
_____
_____

PPEHRC is committed to keeping people alive by any means necessary, and organizing poor and working people to change society so that all people can enjoy the basic necessities of life and share the riches that the world has to offer. We are not a charity, we are a movement. We do this out of commitment, not compensation. Most of us are poor ourselves.

We understand families may have nowhere else to go and are exercising their human right to life, shelter, and warmth. Families will not engage in any illegal drug use or activity at this property. Families will not engage in violence while residing at this property.

As always, parties to PPEHRC work are guided by the 16 Principles of Unity as stated on the website, PoorPeoplesArmy.org.

II. People & orgs involved

The following organizations/people are participating in this agreement as partners. They are committed to working together to ensure the goals of this agreement.

(List project partners)

1. Poor People's Economic Human Rights Campaign / Poor People's Army

Representatives of PPEHRC for the purposes of this agreement are:

_____

_____

Other people or orgs involved:

2. _____

3. _____

4. _____

III. Meetings

This is a movement not a charity non-profit. PPEHRC requires people we assist to go through stages to become a full member/soldier, to learn how to organize and help others in this process. This involves action and education. You show you are becoming a member by what you do, not just what you say. We require individual meetings with parties to this agreement to make sure you are developing and everyone is keeping their agreements to this process and is satisfied. **We want to see you succeed, and we need your help to make us all succeed**. Part of development is:
- Giving back by helping someone else
- A minimum of 2 check-ins per month with PPEHRC leader(s)

- _____

- _____

IV. Signatures

FOR Poor People's Economic Human Rights Campaign / Poor People's Army ("PPEHRC")

Print Name: _____

Signature: _____ Date: _____

Residents in Poor People's Army TAKEOVER HOUSES

I am in this property because I have nowhere else to go and I am exercising my human right to life, shelter, and warmth.
I will not engage in any illegal drug use or activity at this property.
I will not engage in violence while I am residing at this property.

Print Name: _____

Signature: _____ Date: _____

Print Name: _____

Signature: _____ Date: _____

Print Name: _____

Signature: _____ Date: _____

Print Name: _____

Signature: _____ Date: _____

Cheri Honkala, her son Mark Webber, and other homeless families take over the Minneapolis Office of Housing and Urban Development to demand a place to live in 1990. Photo by Joel Severson.

APPENDIX C

Media Featuring the Poor People's Army

Documentaries

Takeover (1992)

Directed and produced by Pamela Yates and Peter Kinoy. Presented by Skylight Pictures. Available at skylight.is/films/takeover/.

"'*We're dying in the streets—that should be against the law' is the no-holds-barred attitude of the homeless men and women who are taking control of their lives and taking over empty houses in Pam Yates and Peter Kinoy's tough, effective film. Funded by Bruce Springsteen, TAKEOVER was shot simultaneously in eight U.S. cities on May 1, 1990 as homeless people risked arrest occupying properties foreclosed by the Federal government.*

An official selection of the Sundance Film Festival, TAKEOVER broadcast on PBS on the P.O.V. series in 1992. Released theatrically at The Film Forum (New York City)." -Skylight Pictures

Homeless Diaries (1996)

Directed and produced by Frances Negrón-Muntaner.

A *documentary about the tent city erected by homeless Philadelphians in the summer of 1995 across from Independence Hall, and the subsequent move of the group to squatting in a nearby unused church.*

Poverty Outlaw (1997)

Directed and produced by Pamela Yates and Peter Kinoy. Presented by Skylight Pictures.

"*Poverty Outlaw is the human drama of women ready to do anything and everything to keep their children and avoid the special penalties of being poor. Veteran documentary filmmakers Pamela Yates and Peter Kinoy bring us this first-person account of one woman's struggle to live on and off welfare.*" -AV Club

Outriders (2000)

Directed and produced by Pamela Yates and Peter Kinoy. Presented by Skylight Pictures and iTVS. Available at skylight.is/films/takeover/.

"*In June 1998, 50 people, mostly women and children, all poor, some homeless, boarded a bus in Philadelphia. They are members of the Kensington Welfare Rights Union—an organization composed of and guided by poor and homeless people—embarking on an odyssey to meet America. For a month they crisscross the country, gathering stories from people who, like themselves, have been cut off welfare or downsized from their jobs. Outriders is the human story of the riders on the New Freedom Bus and the remarkable people they meet.*" -iTVS

The Philadelphia Story (2000)

Directed by Steve Bradshaw. Produced by Television Trust for the Environment. Presented by Bullfrog Films.

"*Cheri Honkala's been homeless, unemployed and—like 44 million of her fellow citizens—doesn't have healthcare. She's one of the workers left behind by the globalized economy. Yet Cheri is a citizen of the United States. In this edition of* Life, *Cheri, executive director of the Kensington Welfare Rights Union, tells the story of what's happened in her hometown, Philadelphia, and warns that the economic boom in the U.S. could yet prove a disturbing model for the rest of the world.*" -Bullfrog Films

Battle for Broad (2001)

Directed by Pamela Yates. Co-produced by Pamela Yates and Gillian Aldrich. Presented by Skylight Pictures and the Media College of the University of the Poor.

The Poor People's Economic Human Rights Campaign plans a march on the 2000 Republican National Convention.

Drug War Reality Tour (2003)

Directed by Stephen Marshall. Presented by the Guerrilla News Network.

"As one of the most innovative and courageous activist networks in the United States, the Kensington Welfare Rights Union (KWRU) has created a legacy of confrontational tactics designed to provoke both the political and social elites who ignore the issues and crises related to poverty. Of these actions, perhaps none is more poignant and effective than The Drug War Reality Tour, in which busloads of tourists are taken on a guided tour of Kensington and shown every aspect of the drug epidemic: from where the drugs arrive to where they are sold and used. Throughout the tour, KWRU members break down facts about the 'drug war' and how forces like police complicity and corporate investment are aiding and using the drug epidemic to drive Kensington's people out of their own neighborhood in order to make room for new urban development.

So get on the bus and experience one of the most controversial and inspiring approaches to social activism ever conceived." -Stephen Marshall

August in the Empire State (2006)

Directed by Keefe Murren and Gabriel Rhodes. Available on Vimeo.

"The 2004 Presidential Election was one of the most divisive moments in recent American history. Amidst the division the Republican Party held its first ever convention in New York City a potent symbol for both President Bush and the local progressives energized to defeat him. August in the Empire State uses the 2004 Republican Convention as a staging ground to explore the intersection between politics activism and media. The filmmakers followed several characters during the months preceding the RNC documenting their preparations as well as their activities during the convention. Cheri Honkala of the Poor People's Economic Human Rights Campaign coordinated her group and marched illegally getting arrested in the process. President of the New York Young Republican Club and aspiring politician Paul Rodriguez campaigned tirelessly for a congressional seat using the convention to meet and network with other young republicans. Journalist Michelle Goldberg covered the convention itself as well as the city's reaction to it. What emerges is an honest snapshot of politics media and culture during an incredibly polarizing time in American history ." -IMDb

Homeless Hero (2009)

By Al Jazeera.

"A homeless mother when she was in her teens, Cheri [Honkala] is the founder of the Kensington Welfare Rights Union, an organisation designed to help the poor and homeless in Philadelphia.

Cheri argues that for too many Americans the homeless are invisible, often being pushed out of cities as part of urban redevelopment plans. The prosperity and progress of shiny new downtown, or city districts, she says, is an illusion that ignores the economic causes of poverty.

With the erosion of U.S. manufacturing jobs, Americans are filing for bankruptcy in record numbers and credit card debt is soaring—leaving more workers just a paycheck away from homelessness.

'In this country there is no safety net and there is no security. You can be ok for one minute and the next day you can be living out on the street and nobody will give a damn about you,' Cheri says.

Homeless Hero is the story of a true American rebel." -Al Jazeera

Books

The Myth of the Welfare Queen: A Pulitzer Prize Winning Journalist's Portrait of Women on the Line (1997)

By David Zucchino. Published by Scribner.

"In this extraordinary first book by a Pulitzer Prize-winning reporter, author David Zucchino sets out to sift through the stereotypes, politics, and pure misinformation about families on welfare. A reporter for The Philadelphia Inquirer, Zucchino gives us an intimate look at Odessa Williams and Cheri Honkala, two 'welfare mothers' from Philadelphia, a city with a disproportionately large number of welfare recipients. He spends the better part of a year with these women, watching as Odessa constructs livable surroundings for herself and her extended family by scavenging and trash picking. Though her character, spirit, and resolve are constantly tested by family crises, she remains the strong and inspir-

ing center of her large—and largely dependent—family.

Zucchino also grows to admire Cheri, a single mother of one son, and a tireless advocate for the rights of the homeless. He watches as she helps one family after another pick up and keep on going. With utter dedication and zeal, and with remarkably little concern for material gains of her own, Cheri battles an inflexible city bureaucracy that in her view makes the already difficult lives of the city's poor nearly impossible.

In this groundbreaking and beautifully written book, Zucchino balances his reporter's objectivity with profound compassion. In seeking to answer the question 'What do welfare mothers do all day?' he uncovers no easy answers but is able to say definitively: 'If there were any Cadillac-driving, champagne-sipping, penthouse-living, welfare queens in Philadelphia, I didn't find them.' " -Jacket

Surviving Poverty: Creating Sustainable Ties Among the Poor (2017)

By Joan Maya Mazelis. Published by NYU Press.

"*Surviving Poverty* carefully examines the experiences of people living below the poverty level, looking in particular at the tension between social isolation and social ties among the poor.

Joan Maya Mazelis draws on in-depth interviews with poor people in Philadelphia to explore how they survive and the benefits they gain by being connected to one another. Half of the study participants are members of the Kensington Welfare Rights Union, a distinctive organization that brings poor people together in the struggle to survive. The mutually supportive relationships the members create, which last for years, even decades, contrast dramatically with the experiences of participants without such affiliation.

In interviews, participants discuss their struggles and hardships, and their responses highlight the importance of cultivating relationships among people living in poverty. Surviving Poverty *documents the ways in which social ties become beneficial and sustainable, allowing members to share their skills and resources and providing those living in similar situations a space to unite and speak collectively to the growing and deepening poverty in the United States. The study concludes that productive, sustainable ties between poor people have an enduring and valuable impact. Grounding her study in current debates about the importance of alleviating poverty, Mazelis proposes new modes of improving the lives of the poor.* Surviving Poverty *is invested in both structural and social change and demonstrates the power support services can have to foster relationships and build sustainable social ties for those living in poverty."* -NYU Press

Scholarly Articles

Noterman, E. (2021). Taking back vacant property. *Urban Geography, 42*(8), 1079–1098.

https://doi.org/10.1080/02723638.2020.1743519

" *'Taking back' has long been a rallying call of urban social movements asserting land rights. This call often involves seeking to ward off dispossession by taking possession. Scholars rethinking property beyond the normative 'ownership model' have explored the seeming paradoxicality of resisting dispossession through legal forms of possession that reproduce deprivation. In this paper, I consider the possibilities for taking back the concept of possession itself by examining claims to 'vacant' property in Philadelphia. I put taking back through a citywide 'land bank' in conversation with the taking over of a poor people's movement that occupies government-owned properties as a means of survival and political mobilization. I argue that outside or on the edge of legal recognition, the effort to take back property functions not as an end in itself, but rather as an explicitly political taking on of the notion of possessive ownership."*

Noterman, E. (2022). Speculating on vacancy. *Transactions of the Institute of British Geographers. 47,* 123-138. 743519

https://doi.org/10.1111/tran.12477

"Property speculation has long served a role in the settler colonial appropriation of land and the racialised uneven development of contemporary cities. This future-oriented approach to property acquisition and management is underpinned by notions of vacancy that erase past and present forms of possession and associate racialised spaces with lack and risk. Efforts to define, represent, and manage the speculative value of 'vacant' properties through predictive mapping work to colonise the future in ways that erase the present and past. In this paper, I reflect on the role of speculative cartographies of property in both reifying and undermining normative urban property regimes. Specifically, I examine the city of Philadelphia's use of cartographic tools to identify 'likely' property vacancy and how they relate to ongoing racialised dispossession. I then turn to consider the potential of speculative (counter) cartographies of property to contribute to new political realities, not just prevailing geographies. To do so, I engage with the work of artists and activists who are using mapmaking grounded in Afrofuturism to reclaim and reimagine the space-times of properties deemed by city officials and developers to be 'empty' or 'wasted.' I suggest that while speculative cartographies of property facilitate the consolidation of liberal property regimes, they also allow for their disruption by revealing their situatedness and contingency—and by facilitating alternative visions of urban futures."

Pastor Keith Collins from Church of the Overcomer marches with members of PPEHRC/PPA to demand homes for the holidays in downtown Philadelphia in 2021. Photo by Erick Jusino Ortiz.

APPENDIX D

Our Philosophy and Perspective on a Changing World (Extended Study Group Version)

"The only real revolutionary, people say, is a man who has nothing to lose. There are millions of poor people in this country who have very little, or even nothing, to lose. If they can be helped to take action together, they will do so with a freedom and a power that will be a new and unsettling force in our complacent national life."

-Dr. Martin Luther King Jr., "Nonviolence and Social Change," 1967

Who We Are

We are building a nonviolent Poor People's Army to keep people alive and to build a cooperative economy and society. This is our mission. We are an organization for present-day conditions, and we are also building an organization that can help for the future. Our Political Context and Philosophy explains the Poor People's Army's analysis of the world and how "takeover houses" are a tactic that has fit into our work. In this extended version of our Political Context and Philosophy, we have included discussion questions for readers to explore in community with others. This philosophy has developed over the course of our 30+ year history, based on our practical lived experiences, our organizing, many mistakes, and much study and discussion with countless individuals across the world.

We are a nonviolent organization based in the United States. Our headquarters is in Philadelphia. We are a movement that came out of the welfare rights and anti-poverty movements of the '60s, '70s, and '80s, and we were founded and are led by poor people, homeless people, people at the bottom that want the power to control our own destinies. (See also our History in the Introduction.) The Poor People's Army has organized communities to advocate for themselves on various issues, used mutual aid and resource sharing to keep poor people alive, fought for and helped people to navigate government benefits and systems, and generally focused on helping people get what they need to survive in a very unfair world. Housing takeovers—finding vacant government-owned houses and moving in homeless families—is one tactic to keep people alive. These actions are central to our organization for today's world. They also challenge people to think of how we could organize a better world.

We are also an organization fighting for humanity's future. We see capitalism, the latest iteration of class conflict, crumbling before our eyes. We know a new kind of fascism is being planned and implemented by the ruling elite to retain their class rule. We know we need to fight for power to create a cooperative society where everyone can get what they need to survive and thrive.

The Ultra-Rich vs. the World

We believe economic conditions today will allow a cooperative society to exist within our lifetimes. We live in a world where it is possible for every human being to have the basic necessities of life and live comfortably. We know that the ultra-rich and corporations will not willingly share the wealth and resources the world has to offer. They undemocratically hoard the wealth, the world's abundant resources, and the incredible productive powers that could allow for all humans to flourish.

We understand that the ultra-rich—a class that rules society, a ruling class—are at war with us daily. Their class uses a variety of means to fight against poor and working people. We are an Army that seeks to unite our class. We identify our class as unemployed, underemployed, working, the so-called "middle class," and the professional class—anyone who does not control the way the system runs. We identify the ultra-rich, with the exception of some class traitors, as the main benefactors and controllers of the current system. The ultra-rich are not people with a couple million dollars; they are fantastically wealthy and control how the economy operates.

There are multiple publically available resources documenting who the ultra-rich are and how much their wealth has continued to skyrocket while people go hungry. According to the report "Inequality Kills: The unparalleled action needed to combat unprecedented inequality in the wake of COVID 19", published in 2022 by Oxfam, "The world's ten richest men more than doubled their fortunes from $700 billion to $1.5 trillion—at a rate of $15,000 per second or $1.3 billion a day—during the first two years of a pandemic that has seen the incomes of 99 percent of humanity fall and over 160 million more people forced into poverty."

This is not a conspiratorial, shadowy group of figures—the names of these men are publicly available. According to Forbes' 2024 Billionaires List, the 14 richest people in the world have over $100 billion each. These are their names: Bernard Arnault of France, Elon Musk of the United States, Jeff Bezos of the United States, Mark Zuckerberg of the United States, Larry Ellison of the United States, Warren Buffett of the United States, Bill Gates of the United States, Steve Ballmer of the United States, Mukesh Ambani of India, Larry Page of the United States, Sergey Brin of the United States, Michael Bloomberg of the United States, Amancio Ortega of Spain, and Carlos Slim Helú of Mexico.

We call these people and the rest of the ultra-rich the "ruling class" because they effectively control the economy—making decisions about how much food is grown, how housing markets operate, how the healthcare system runs, and more. They own thousands of hospitals, they own the majority of farmland in the country, and they are trying to own the water. They help write laws and use their money and power to undermine our so-called democracy. Many of them are politicians themselves. They have bought out and corporatized the media and culture that shapes our perception of what's possible. They rule over society. The ruling class owns, controls, and uses corporations to do a lot of this work. Some call them *capitalists* because they control the system of capitalism.

Meanwhile, the vast majority of Americans do not own corporations, do not own businesses that can decide how food and medicines are made, how housing is planned, how water is kept clean, or how educational resources are created for our children. Most Americans have to work to survive, run small businesses or side hustles, or other means to get their basic needs met. According to "The State of U.S. Wealth Inequality," a 2023 report conducted by the U.S. Federal Reserve, these people—the bottom 50%—control less than 3% of the wealth. In fact, the bottom 90% control little more than 30% of the wealth. This system—the ruling class exploiting the working class—is capitalism.

A Turning Point: Automation and the End of Human Labor

This capitalist system that keeps people poor or running every moment of their lives has come to a turning point: unprecedented innovation alongside "unprecedented inequality", as the Oxfam report says. The system is based on competition and creating new innovations. Though it exploits and hurts people, it also races to build up technology and creates marvelous advances in science and industry. If corporations wish to survive, they cannot stop innovating and competing, finding new ways to make money. But in that innovation, they have created new tools that are seeds for a new society. Computers, robots, science, and other technologies are producing more and more things *with less and less necessary human labor*. It was only around 60 years ago that the first microchips and robot arms were introduced to the production of goods. So much has changed in 60 years, and we can't begin to comprehend the changes that are coming in the next 60 years. In the beginning, it was physical labor that was assisted and then replaced by machines. In the modern day, intellectual work and specialized work have been added to that list.

These new advances are making all human work precarious—no one can count on their job being there in the future. According to "A future that works: Automation, employment, and productivity," a 2017 report by McKinsey & Company, 1.1 billion workers across the globe could be replaced with currently existing tools of automation, impacting $15.8 trillion in wages. Even "professional" employment that appeared untouchable by automation and extremely wealth-producing—such as the work of doctors, professors, actors, writers, and lawyers—is becoming precarious through the advance of technology. World class surgeons are now assisting robots doing the actual surgeries, learning devices and online courses are taking over huge sections of educational markets, and the legal world is implementing discovery and brief-drafting software. Actors and writers in Hollywood have gone on strike in an attempt to prevent automation from ruining their careers. Some are hurting now because of labor-replacing technology; some will hurt later. We all have the potential for our labor to be replaced by machines.

To be clear, it's not the technology itself that is the danger. The fear and danger is us not being able to pay for food, housing, and healthcare. The fear and danger is that we don't control how technology is used. This is an antagonism that is being created today and that cannot be resolved in the current system. We see an unprecedented world of possibility based on the productive capacity in the machines, computers, and automation that humans have built. Things that seemed impossible, like feeding, clothing, and sheltering the entire human population, are now easily possible. Scarcity only plagues us because the people lack power. Not power through Congress, or power through entrepreneurship, or entering corporate boardrooms, but economic power by controlling how we make and distribute all goods and services.

Technology is merely a tool for humans to use. But in today's unjust society, the ruling class uses these tools against the vast majority of people only for their own benefit. The ultra-rich are using these tools to strip away the utility of human work. In our contemporary world, human work is intrinsically linked to human value. The possibility exists for a society where everyone has the basic necessities of life, where war and famine are prevented, and where problems are collectively solved. Computers, science, and machines can allow for this. We also acknowledge that humans must enact a better harmony with the Earth and mother nature. We can look to lessons of Native peoples who have always centered this relationship. But it can only happen if the people collectively own and control technology. The Poor People's Army hopes to be a force to unite people around a new vision for taking control of technology, of taking control of the basic necessities of life for all people, of sharing and developing a new system for all people.

Capitalism is Ending Itself

While we understand the allure of "fighting against capitalism," a system that has hurt so many people and is built on genocide, white supremacy, and patriarchy, we want to be clear that capitalism is *already dying*. We don't need to proclaim ourselves "anticapitalist" (even as we philosophically may be)—we no longer need to use ideology alone to convince people to create revolutionary change. Capitalism is in the revolutionary process of *ending itself* by innovating technologies that will render it obsolete. We don't need people to be ideological revolutionaries. We need people to understand concretely what is occuring in society and the economy. The ruling class sees how capitalism is shifting into something new, a society where human exploitation is not central. The ruling class is thinking of ways to adapt to a society centered around automation, but they are not thinking of it in a way that will benefit all humanity. They are using all their think tanks, military power, and money to brainstorm ways to center the economy around robot labor while retaining political power over 99.9% of the rest of us. The expansion of AI into arts and entertainment in a way that co-opts human labor (and even human likenesses) is a prominent example of this; there are many others.

The only thing worse than being exploited is not being needed. Capitalism requires exploitation of the vast majority of humanity. If society runs primarily on automation instead of human labor, then the ruling class will seek other ways to keep us divided, distracted, numb, isolated, and self-destructive. Ultimately, they may be faced with more extreme solutions to keeping their power. But by displacing more and more human labor, corporations that sell products can't get their profits if people can't afford to buy them. The system comes to a grinding halt if people can't buy stuff.

While the death of capitalism is causing the ruling class to begin to implement fascist controls, this era also creates fertile ground for something new to grow. Whether our new world prioritizes care, focuses on our collective well-being, and keeps power in the hands of the people depends on how effectively we can organize and unite the class of people who now find themselves at the economic margins. This new revolutionary class, growing by the day, will ultimately need to take power in order to survive.

Our Army seeks to keep people alive as we are attacked daily and maintaining a basic standard of living gets harder and harder in this time of major economic transition. As we keep people alive, we engage them in political education to see past divisive ideologies that have pitted them against their neighbors.

As capitalism crumbles further, poor and working people will continue to endure violence at the hands of the police, the courts, prisons, and detention centers. We endure violence from a healthcare system that excludes us, that ignores our mental health, that treats our addictions and sorrows as personal failures instead of systemic ones. We endure violence from social workers and systems put in place to criminalize poverty and punish poor parents by breaking up families, by removing children from their homes, and by imprisoning and punishing poor parents and caregivers. We continue to endure violence from corporations that influence and control laws that make us work ourselves to the bone or starve while they reap higher and higher profits. These same corporations poison our water, air, and soil, creating the conditions for mass extinction and climate catastrophes that impact billions of people across the globe.

History as Inspiration

While the world at times seems hopeless for so many people, we look back to systems of oppression in the past that fell under their own weight—systems of brutal slavery and oppression, monarchs that people thought were ordained by God, empires that spanned the globe, and many instances of colonialism. We study the way human society has transformed as a result of new tools and people's revolutions. In every existing society there are seeds for a future society. Although humans themselves impact great revolutionary change in society and politics, we also understand how tools and technological advancements in the economy always create revolutionary potential.

In the times of kings and queens, serfs and peasants and merchants, revolutions did not start with people deciding kings and queens must be overthrown. It started because some of the common people working as merchants built up better and better tools. The beginning of mechanized tools and industry began a revolution in the economy that would eventually end feudalism and monarchies, because it created an unresolvable antagonism in society at the time. Merchants using these new tools became the first leaders of industry—business or corporate leaders as we think of them today. As they built larger and larger workshops and factories, and began hiring other people to work for them, this new class of business owners was a threat to the power of kings and queens. There could not be two ruling classes, and the growth of industry could not be stopped. So the leaders of industry were forced to fight against the monarchies for "freedom" to continue expanding industry and their power over the still-existing peasant class and emerging working class.

Ideals of freedom, liberty, and democracy were developed around these new economic changes, and social revolutions occurred because of them. People of all kinds rallied around the concepts of liberty and freedom, and the very real brutalities of kings and queens, but most of those revolutions ended feudalism and created capitalism (a new system of exploitation). We are familiar with the phrases "all men are created equal" from the American Revolution and "liberty, equality, fraternity" from the French Revolution, but we know these new governments still repeated systems of exploitation despite the change in structures of power. At the time there was not enough to adequately take care of all people, even in places where so-called socialism/communism was implemented. We admire common people who fought and organized to rise up against oppression. But we also see that technology began the revolution.

We can also learn a lesson from the ways that Western capitalism dramatically expanded its domination internationally after WWII. When advances in technology made the specific locations of factories less restricted as well as increasing profits, rather than sharing that profit with workers, corporations moved their factories and operations from "developed" countries to the Global South in search of cheaper labor. This left millions of workers in the U.S. jobless, while continuing the exploitative legacy of colonialism for the people in the Global South forced into even more inhumane working conditions, and forcing people in the U.S. to take the jobs that came to replace manufacturing, which were largely low-paying service jobs. Booming cities transformed into post-industrial wastelands in a decade or two. During that time, Black people, Indigenous people, and other people of color bore the brunt of job losses. Today, we are hurtling towards the edge of a similar cliff, but now white and middle class people who were previously privileged are now destined to join the permanently unemployed. Automation threatens all jobs. According to a June 2023 report by "outplacement" firm Challenger, Gray, & Christmas, Inc., layoffs increased by 315% between May of 2022 and 2023, and it's estimated that 4,000 jobs were replaced in one month by AI.

How We Win

The antagonism of today is here: people need work to survive in this system, but more and more work is being done by technology. If people can't work, they will need another way to get food, clothing, housing, water. As the recursive self-destruction of capitalism expands into more and more sectors, the hope for humanity is that we no longer need to convince people of an ideology to fight the system. They will be forced to fight for their survival across racial lines, across religious lines, across all human differences as the material realities brought on by this moment become more and more evident if they can see this reality that humanity faces.

Certainly, ruling class ideologies of white supremacy and patriarchy, etc. will continue to live in the minds of people. But they will be forced to reckon with the reality of being thrown out of the economy in a way that will supersede those divisions. And we as organizers need to work with them to see past the various lenses they've been given to what is really going on.

There is more manufactured scarcity than ever, and at the same time there is more and more real abundance than ever. This antagonism could lead to either fascism and total control by today's ruling class, or a new system where people control the basic necessities of life for ourselves, and decide together how technology can best serve humanity.

We understand that poor and working people must find a way to unite during the difficult transition that lies in the years ahead. We also know that it will take organizing to build the forces capable of ultimately getting rid of inequality. We need to share this vision, to educate people and empower them. We need to identify the potential of the beautiful world that awaits us. We need to build our class's identity and consciousness more than anything. We need to meet people where they're at, and catch people when they're down. We need to be mindful that people will be most willing to see this potential when they are thrown out of the current system.

One way we can build our side is to increase activities that point out the contradictions and antagonisms in society today. We can't just "fight back" against isolated disastrous changes, or organize in silos that only take on injustices facing one section of the population, of the new class of people cast aside by our changing world. We have to understand how all oppression and repression is connected. We must focus on collective solutions, on the control of how goods are produced and distributed and shared. We can take every opportunity to highlight contradictions and antagonisms by taking back empty houses for homeless people, taking back empty land for communities' use, by distributing free food instead of forcing people to be exploited in order to get their needs met. We can call out when our government can find billions of dollars instantly for wars but is gridlocked for any meaningful change at home, when it imposes sanctions on regimes abroad and does not recognize the sanctions it imposes against poor and working people in the U.S. through denial of benefits and withholding of the basic necessities of life. We can use portions of the system to expose the system: running for office as independent political candidates and challenging the dead-end corporatization of the Democratic and Republican parties. We can use existing organizations and institutions that are willing to look outside the system for change, we can create new organizations and groupings, and we can expose organizations propping up the status quo.

A major tactic and community-building tool we have used is housing takeovers. We take every opportunity to build unity by doing our best to catch people when they are thrown out of the system—when they are outsourced, downsized, or kicked out of their homes or apartments. We do our best to assist people when they can't get access to decent healthcare or detox on demand, when they are bankrupted by hospital bills or denied treatment by insurance companies. We are there when they can't reunite with their children, or the state is threatening to take their kids away simply because they are poor. These are our people, a new class. And if we can grow the consciousness of this new class, then it will be possible to transform society together. We can break down the false political ideologies of "liberal" and "conservative" used to divide us, and unify the bottom to come for the top.

We must point out false opportunities, misdirection, and dead end roads for our side. We have to expose who the monarchs, slavemasters, and colonists are in this era, and we cannot work with them or their allies.

We ourselves—the bottom, this new revolutionary class, the majority of humans being displaced by automation—are the only hope for humanity. There is a role for all of us.

We hope this book is the first in a series of lessons, tactics, and philosophies that we intend to share to help our class fight to keep ourselves alive today, and to unite for the battles ahead.

We are the leaders that we are looking for. Let's seize this moment.

-Poor People's Army, Spring 2024

Discussion Questions

1. What do you know about the welfare rights and anti-poverty movement? Where could you go to learn more?

2. What special experiences do the "organized poor" like the Poor People's Army have to teach? How can their life experiences and organizing experience benefit larger sections of the population?

3. What does "ruling class" mean? Who are these people and what are their relations to corporations and local, state, and federal governments?

4. Who is the richest person you know? How far away is that person from being a billionaire? What does that tell you about the way our society is structured?

5. What myths have you been taught about who has access to wealth and power? How can we break down conspiracy theories while building our understanding of the unequal distribution of resources in the world?

6. If science and technology does not ever stop advancing, does it mean that every job could be automated at some point in the future? What are some jobs that used to be done by humans that are now done by machines?

7. How has technology been used to harm people in your life, neighborhood, or community?

8. How could technology be used to help people in your life, neighborhood, or community in new ways? What would need to change for that to happen?

9. How do you hear people around you talk about capitalism today? How has that changed from when you were younger?

10. What are the opportunities in this moment where capitalism is in crisis? What are the dangers?

11. What does it mean that we don't need to convince people of an anticapitalist ideology? How do we ground our organizing and politics in the concrete realities of people's lives and show them that an economic revolution is already underway?

12. What examples of historical revolutionary change have you learned about? What caused that change to happen?

13. How do narratives around societal progress prioritize individual "heroes" over collaborative organizing and community efforts? Where can you go to learn about the ways that progress happened collectively?

15. What moments in the past feel connected or similar to this moment? What lessons can we learn from those times?

16. Who and what gives you hope right now? How can you organize around those people and inspirations?

17. How is the housing takeover movement connected to the bigger movement for a cooperative society?

18. How can you take the lessons from this philosophy and this book as a whole and apply them in your own organizing?

Cheri Honkala and her son Guillermo Santos at a homeless encampment in Tennessee celebrating the anniversary of the 1968 Mule March in 2005. Photo by Harvey Finkle.